I am in this world
I travel in the air
I was not born in the earth
I was born in the sky
My father is the North Cloud
My mother, the South Cloud.

I have come to call you from the ocean.
You will be needed in this world.
When trees come, you will quicken them.
When people come, you will comfort them.
You will make the life of the people.
Do not refuse me
I am not deceiving you.

from *Annikadel*, C. HART MERRIAM

Almost Ancestors

Almost Ancestors

SIERRA CLUB

The First Californians

by Theodora Kroeber and Robert F. Heizer

edited by F. David Hales

SAN FRANCISCO NEW YORK LONDON

The Sierra Club, founded in 1892 by John Muir, has devoted itself to the study and protection of scenic resources and wild places around the world. Sierra Club publications are part of the nonprofit effort the club carries on as a public trust. The club is affiliated with the International Union for Conservation, the National Resources Council of America, the Conservation Foundation, and the Federation of Western Outdoor Clubs. There are chapters in California, the Pacific Northwest, the Great Basin, the Southwest, the Great Lakes region, on the Atlantic Seaboard, Hawaii, and Alaska. Participation is invited in the program to enjoy and preserve wilderness, wildlife, forests, and streams. *Main office: Mills Tower, San Francisco. Other offices: 15 E. 53rd. St., New York; 235 Massachusetts Ave., NE, Washington D.C.; 6 Langley St., London W.C.2; 427 West 5th St., Los Angeles; and in Seattle, Washington, and Albuquerque, New Mexico.*

We gratefully acknowledge permission to reprint material from books by Lord Snowdon and A. L. Kroeber copyrighted by them in the years shown and published by the firms indicated:

London, copyright 1955, reprinted by permission of Jarrold & Sons Ltd.

Handbook of the Indians of California, copyright 1925, 1958, 1967. Reprinted by permission of California Book Co., Ltd., Berkeley.

Photographs 42, 56, 64, and 97 are reproduced by courtesy of the American Museum of Natural History.

Publisher's Note: The book is set in Centaur and Arrighi by Mackenzie & Harris, Inc., San Francisco. It was lithographed on Oxford Duoset by H. S. Crocker Co., Inc., Cincinnati, Ohio and bound in Columbia Mills Fictionette by A. Horowitz & Son, Clifton, New Jersey. The design is by David Brower.

PUBLICATIONS COMMITTEE, 1967-1968
AUGUST FRUGÉ, *Chairman;* CHARLES B. HUESTIS, MARTIN LITTON
GEORGE MARSHALL, WILLIAM E. SIRI
EDGAR WAYBURN (*ex officio, President of the club*);
DAVID BROWER, *Executive Director;* HUGH NASH, *Secretary;*
CLIFFORD J. RUDDEN, *Controller*

1. LAKE MIWOK, Oleyome subtribe; photo 1906

2. KAROK; Sandy Bar Bob; photo 1921

Contents

ONE HUNDRED SEVENTEEN PHOTOGRAPHS

FOREWORD

MAN HAS SUCCEEDED all too well in extirpating wildness without quite knowing what that wildness means, to itself, to other living things, to him. For several years, now, the Sierra Club has been singling out some elements of wildness that seem beautiful by today's standards, and that the club thinks will be important by any standards. Books have been published to celebrate wild places, to let people know about them, to elicit protection of the irreplaceables, to urge that civilization flow around the wilderness and not over it, to suggest that this wilderness holds answers to questions man has not yet learned how to ask. Science, technology, and genius can sustain man and his works outside.

One of those books was about Navajo wildlands, and we managed to publish such a book without a single Indian showing, but with much of the country beautifully in view. Now it is turnabout—Indians, and no country at all. The faces here represent California tribes that white men exterminated—tribes whose elements were slowly gathered together, each one discrete, each one alive on a living land, and each one now gone. Empathy may not rise high when a piece of wild land perishes, but when a whole tribe vanishes, when fifty tribes disappear forever, we may well think that there but for the grace of God go we.

Perhaps these faces can be symbols for us, can make more poignant the tragedy we are inflicting on living things less like ourselves. Perhaps we can wonder a moment what it might be like, for example, to be the last man on earth who could speak French. Man has been forgiven often for knowing not what he does. For the kind of error that wiped out this kind of uniqueness there cannot be much more forgiveness. There isn't enough of it left, any more, to let die or to kill or to poison or to pave over. Too many species are down to the last that speak their language, and organic wholeness will be lessened when they go, on whatever part of this planet they inhabit. What lessens them diminishes us, for there is no island.

DAVID BROWER

San Francisco, June 25, 1968   *Executive Director, Sierra Club*

8

3. SOUTHERN MAIDU (?);

photo *ca.* 1850

PREFACE

THIS IS A BOOK of pictures of faces, the faces of some one hundred Indians of California. We, the authors, have in several ways been long concerned with the anthropological study of those ancient and fascinating people and this book grows from a desire to communicate something of their look and nature.

With F. S. Archer's discovery in 1851 of the wet-collodion process for fixing an image on a light-sensitive plate, travelers, journalists, and students were soon carrying a camera as well as notebook and pencil: a moment of native history was imprinted on glass and celluloid for all time. It is from such records that our faces come.

On this page is the earliest picture we have of a California Indian. Frank A. Robertson found this daguerreotype in a pile of trash in the attic of an old house in Los Angeles and gave it to the Southwest Museum. The Museum believes it was made perhaps as early as 1850, and that it is of a Southern Maidu Indian, because the unusual headdress he is wearing belonged to that tribe. Note the cylindrical carved ornaments in the ears and the bundle of arrows and bow in his lap.

Pictures are taken differently today from the way they were a hundred years ago, or even fifty. Says Lord Snowdon of his pictures of Londoners (*London,* Tony Armstrong Jones, 1958), "I used a small camera, little apparatus, and no artificial lighting at all, because this seems to me the only way a photographer can hope to keep himself out of the scene. Someone who buries his head in a black cloth or an enormous view-finder may think he is invisible, but he's oppressively there to everyone else." Alas, the cameraman is most oppressively there in each of our pictures. By the time the camera had become small and speedy, and photographers had learned to record unposed unself-conscious moments vibrant with barely arrested motion, there was no longer an indigenous way of life to record.

If the pictures here fail to be perfectly sharp the reason is that most of them were taken by nonprofessionals who failed to set the distance scale properly; if they are blurred it is because the subject moved and there was no opportunity for a retake. In short, the photographs are what they happen to be. We have few full-length pictures, and often not even the hands are shown. With few exceptions the faces are either straight front or straight profile; they are posed and stiff and formal. Some of the most typically Indian of our faces look un-Indian because the hair is no longer done in native style and the clothes are those of the conqueror, a style which at its best tended to the heavy and the clumsy. And the Indians had little opportunity to wear this style at its best or even to see it. Pioneer and missionary custom required that the body be almost entirely concealed. Any discarded shirt and pants satisfied these requirements for the native men. And the women were often in the shapeless and concealing Mother Hubbards that white people have favored for their warmer-skinned sisters wherever they have been and taken it upon themselves to improve the "savages."

Perhaps you can in imagination dress the people of our pictures in their own clothes. The women would be in full skirts coming a few inches below the knee, which allowed them to sit modestly on the ground or floor. Sometimes these would be of deerskin but on most occasions they would be made of rushes or of the shredded bark of willow or cedar or redwood. The breasts would be bare but around the neck would be many strings of shell and stone and bone beads. The hair would be parted in the middle and hanging in two sleek plaits over the shoulders or down the back, tied with ribbons of rabbit or mink or some other fur. The men would wear only an apron-belt of deer hide. Their long hair would be in a brush tied at the nape of the neck or worn on top of the head encased in a fine net. Both men and women would wear feather or fur capes in cold weather and sandals or moccasins for wet or snowy days. The children, the run-abouts at least, would wear no clothes at all.

Almost the only truly native hairdress our pictures preserve is the short, singed-off hair worn as a sign of mourning; this style is identical for men and women and at times makes the old women look to us like men. We abandoned all but one or two of the few pictures we had of Indians in native dress. Such pictures are seldom wholly authentic and the wearers, as unused to the clothes as one of us, have the self-conscious costumed look of masqueraders. In one such picture, the costumes and weapons are ethnologically correct, but the three young and lively Mohaves who had posed for it, hunters and potential fighters, are holding their bows awkwardly—no doubt the photographer placed them so—and their expressions are withdrawn, tentative, uncomfortable.

Or see the pictures below. They are of Alice and Robert Spott, two of the handsomest and most interesting and vivid of any people in this book. Their clothes are accurate except for the long-sleeved undershirt Alice is wearing that wholly negates the style, and we are allowed only a glimpse of her pendant-hung, full deerskin skirt. Robert, too, should be in full length and his hair, military short, destroys the set and look of the red woodpecker crown. Both of them are deprecatory; the sparkle and animation natural to them is quenched.

It is not to be assumed that the beards in our pictures were grown in imitation of the white man. Indians have a lighter growth of face and body hair than do Caucasians and usually they pluck out mustache and beard hairs with tweezers as do many Oriental people. But an Indian not infrequently allowed a mustache or beard to grow.

Many of our plates and negatives are scratched; and more often than not we have had to work from a faded print. With all these limitations, you may ask, why offer so flawed and partial a record? It is all the record there is and although frontier artists' drawings, engravings, and paintings tell much they fail to reproduce characteristic features, proportions, or expressions. We believe you will see through the pictures, imperfect as they are, to the living human beings who sat for them. And to further your understanding of them, we devote some space to an account which will at least touch upon the prehistory and history of the Californians, how they lived, what they thought and believed, what made them alike or different from one another and from Indians outside California. Our quotes are from the *Handbook of the Indians of California* by Alfred Kroeber or from other ethnographic descriptive accounts. The quotations are in the present tense, known as the "ethnological present," in which an ethnologist reports data that he has got directly from a living informant.

Regretfully, in our own voice we must use the past tense.

THEODORA KROEBER
ROBERT F. HEIZER

4. YUROK; Alice Frank Spott, age 27; photo 1907

FACES MIRROR
THE OLD LOOK,
COMELY, SERENE, HUMANE

5. YUROK; Robert Frank Spott; photo *ca.* 1932

12

There above, there above
On the roof of the Earthlodge
Of the south

Spirits dance
And fall

Flowers bend
On their stems.

I. A WORLD NEARLY CONTEMPORARY

A VANISHED GARDEN

THE HISTORY OF MAN is in a sense the story of a succession through time of an uncounted number of worlds that differ, little or much, one from another in their period and place, in their plants and animals, in their people and customs. Of past worlds that had no writing, some flourished and died and are gone—we know nothing at all about them. Yet other worlds left traces which the archeologist discovers and by the act of discovery literally recreates. Then there are worlds so nearly contemporary that some few of their people, still living, pass on by word of mouth to an anthropologist, an explorer, or a missionary some account of their language and customs and beliefs, which, being recorded, preserve at least their ultimate moment before extinction and register them in the long roster of civilizations.

In the middle stretch of the long Pacific coast, and screened to the east by the Sierra Nevada, lay a congeries of such small worlds in the area that the early Spanish explorers, who first came upon it, named California. Although so recent as to be almost contemporary, the native culture no longer exists there. The living descendants of the native peoples are the great-grandchildren of those Indians who survived invasion and they know of their ancestral civilization only by hearsay and to the extent that a grandmother, a great-grandfather, or an old aunt taught them when they were young. They may know a few words of the tongue of their forefathers which will serve to identify the linguistic family to which they belonged; they will occasionally have a speaking knowledge sufficient to reconstruct the grammar and syntax and a considerable vocabulary. The thrice-removed memory of the California Indians of a time when the Old Ones, their ancestors, were the sole possessors of the land, lingers on here and there in out-of-the-way places.

Gunnar Myrdal, the Swedish anthropologist, classifies Americans as "real" and "new." The real Americans are those copper-colored peoples known as Indians since Christopher Columbus miscalculated his whereabouts in 1492. At some time in a prehistory whose beginnings become ever more remote in time as archeological evidence builds—ten thousand, twenty thousand years ago are now conservative estimates—a Mongoloid people began migrating from Asia into the Americas, coming by way of the land bridge across Bering Strait, their descendants gradually penetrating to the extremes of the two unpeopled continents and so becoming the scattered seed plots of the indigenous, ancient population of the Americas.

The new Americans are the late-comers, Caucasians from Europe, Orientals from eastern Asia, and Negroes from Africa. The farthest stretch of the history of these new Americans is a mere four and a half centuries, one or two centuries being the limit of their ancestors' presence in the country for most of them. It is important to remember that the Indians were racially and culturally different from any of the new Americans, whose response to these differences, at least on the part of the Anglo-Saxons, was an attitude at once detached and impersonalized—particularly useful when it came to dispossessing the Indians of their land or slaughtering them: no trace of identification with them stood in the way. The Indian was a person apart, human but uncivilized, who if he did not voluntarily stand aside for the advance of "civilization" should be made to do so.

The conscience of government, whether Spanish, Dutch, English, or after 1776 the United States, was eased by the drawing up of treaties with certain of the Indians. These were meant to make the taking of the land legal, to "quiet title." With a few or a score of these treaties in hand, no government hesitated to make all land available to new settlers. Certain arbitrarily reserved small parcels of marginal land were kept for the dispossessed Indians, and if the Indians resisted having their good land wrested from them, and themselves removed to an unknown place, military action was instituted against them. Nor was it much the custom to take prisoners in these "wars." Should the invaders renege on the treaties, the Indians had no recourse, outside rebellion, but to complain to an officialdom distant, usually unsympathetic and pressed by nearer problems. So went the conquest of North America. It began on the Atlantic seaboard, proceeding westward across the Mississippi River and the Plains, over the Rocky Mountains and across the Great Basin and finally over the Sierra Nevada, there to meet and replace the earlier and partial conquest of the Pacific Coast by the Spaniards.

A VANISHED
GARDEN

EVEN TODAY one may sometimes overhear two old Indians speaking confidentially together in the aboriginal tongue.

Or come upon a woman grinding and leaching acorns in preparation for the family supper.

Or see a young Indian woman seat herself on the ground, bend her legs and make a circle of her calico skirts in the single easy motion with which her great-grandmother once seated herself and spread her full bark skirt.

Or be present when Indian men sing some of the old songs and dance a few steps from a World Renewal dance, in nostalgia for a ritual and a belief less real than a dream.

Flickering sparks, these, of a way of life alien, natural, belonging.

6. MOHAVE; photo *ca.* 1900

A VANISHED
GARDEN

With the coastal voyage of the Spanish sailor, Cabrillo, in 1542 the native period, the prehistoric one, began to come to a close. In 1579, Sir Francis Drake spent five weeks probably in the anchorage sheltered behind Point Reyes, now called Drake's Bay, repairing his ship the "Golden Hind." During this time he was in touch with the Miwok Indians who lived there and who were the first California Indians to have contact with English-speaking people. By 1769 Spain was building missions in California, the Spanish conquerors envisioning a society there like the one fairly well established in Mexico: a heathen population brought under the protection of Church and Crown and forming a broad peon base above which, pyramidally, would be a mestizo class and, topping that, a Creole aristocracy, a society of conquerors and their children.

To this end new missions were filled with Indians rounded up from villages beside the sea, from valleys, from foothill country, from any nearby area. This was done without reference to tribe, tongue, or personal willingness, without concern that Indians from different places spoke mutually unintelligible languages, were total strangers to each other, and could not form a society forcibly thrown together as they were. Whole nations, languages, and cultures were in this manner wiped out. It was not the intent of the Spaniards to decimate a population upon whom their vision of the future depended. But they did not learn in time the temperament of the Indian, which was such that uprooted, enslaved, stripped of his identity and separated from his kind, he would choose death to life. Diseases introduced by the Spanish (and later by the Anglo-Saxons) killed scores of thousands of Indians; others by the hundreds, perhaps the thousands, no one knows how many, willed themselves to die, there being no longer a reason for living.

Mexican independence from Spain in 1821 brought a new ruling group into California for a few years; with the signing of the Treaty of Guadalupe-Hidalgo in 1848 at the conclusion of the Mexican War California became a part of the United States: the Anglo-Saxon phase of invasion was at hand and conquest took on new and more ruthless aspects. Spanish society, on the one hand, was hierarchic, feudal, and ecclesiastic, one in which the Indians would fit on a lower stratum. Society in the United States, on the other hand, was already thoroughly committed to a middle-class ideal and ideology: it was mercantile and fast becoming industrialized; its religion Protestant, its ethic Puritan. It was experientially and imaginatively unprepared to find a place within it for the Indian. The Spanish in California were always few compared with the Indians, but the Gold Rush brought pioneers in overwhelming numbers across the former barrier of the Sierra Nevada and around Cape Horn. The Anglo-Saxons made no place for the Indians in their dreams of wealth and expansion; they set out to enslave them, herd them onto reservations out of the way, let them die, or better, kill them, exterminate them. By and large, they succeeded. Within ten years of California's becoming a state, only an occasional tatter of Indian life remained more or less intact, much as in a burnt-over area a piece of green forest may have survived the flames that blew above and beyond it. In their ignorance and their intolerant racism, the white men called the Californians "Diggers," regarding them as scarcely human. Indian-killers were tolerated, their profession considered an honorable one by many of their fellows.

We have no way of determining precisely how many Indians there were when the state was discovered by the Spaniards. These early contacts were brief and generally friendly, and noses were not counted. Scholars have come to the conclusion that about 300,000 natives occupied the 156,000 square miles of California's surface in 1500 A.D. (We are quoting the highest of the estimates.) We know that by 1850 there were only 100,000 surviving Indians; by 1870, 30,000; in 1880, 20,000; and in 1910, 16,000, after which date the numbers have slowly increased to about 30,000 in 1960. Thus four and a quarter centuries of history have passed since the native Indian world first came into contact with European peoples and cultures. The process of succession has now run its full course. We who live in California today occupy land that belonged to the Indians since time beyond memory. The land, however violated, endures; its natal culture wholly obliterated, its natal peoples nearly so.

The question is asked: How is it that a way of life and a people could be made so wholly to disappear as did the California Indian? One anthropological answer is: Ignorance makes of a man a fear-full animal whose response to alien eyes, skin color, dress, and custom is hostile, whose single impulse is to stamp out, to obliterate from sight and consciousness a world view that contravenes his own. And conquerors have a way of being not only brave and adventurous but ignorant and benighted, and racist as well, which qualities the beneficiaries of conquest tend to take for granted. No one troubled to name what was happening in California a hundred years ago genocide. It was only with the Second World War, after a Lidice, a Coventry, the almost successful attempt to wipe out a whole culture and religion in places like Auschwitz and Buchenwald, that the true meaning of the word, of the act, and of its inhumanity bore in upon the collective conscience.

But, besides those who were responsible for the genocide of Californians,

A VANISHED GARDEN

A VANISHED GARDEN

there were among the newcomers those who were not ignorant, not benighted, but who were humane, knowledgeable, and perceptive of the exotic, the beautiful, the tragic. Some of them wrote letters or kept journals telling of the people and the land. It is from these records, from the more than sixty years of anthropological fieldwork with surviving Indians, and from the archeological excavations which bring to light that part of the story held beneath the surface of the earth, that a considerable body of California history and prehistory is now on record.

LAST SURVIVORS

WITH THE DEATH OF EACH OF THESE INDIVIDUALS
THERE DISAPPEARED FROM THE FACE OF THE EARTH
THE LAST LIVING REPRESENTATIVE OF
A PEOPLE
A LANGUAGE
AN INDEPENDENT TRIBELET-STATE
A PARTICULAR WAY OF INTERPRETING LIFE
   AND ITS MYSTERIES

THE LAST SURVIVOR CONFRONTS
AN ABSOLUTE OF LONELINESS

HE POSSESSES TOTAL IDENTITY ONLY TO HIMSELF

7. FERNANDEÑO; Rogerio Rocha, born 1801, died 1904

8. COSTANOAN OF MISSION SAN JUAN BAUTISTA;
Barbara Salorsano, age *ca.* 60; photo 1902

9. WINTUN, Napa tribelet; photo 1927

10. SOUTHERN MAIDU; Blind Tom; photo 1905

11. YOKUTS, Yachicumni subtribe;
Joe Guzman; photo 1934

22

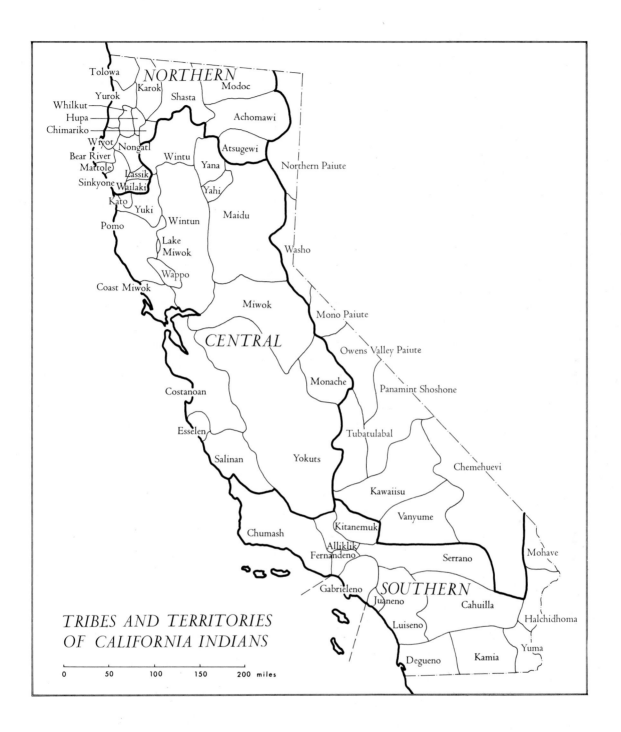

TRIBES AND TERRITORIES
OF CALIFORNIA INDIANS

Tolowa
NORTHERN
Karok
Yurok
Shasta
Modoc
Whilkut
Hupa
Achomawi
Chimariko
Wiyot
Nongatl
Atsugewi
Bear River
Wintu
Northern Paiute
Mattole
Yana
Lassik
Sinkyone
Wailaki
Yahi
Kato
Yuki
Wintun
Maidu
Pomo
Lake
Miwok
Washo
Wappo
Coast Miwok
Miwok
CENTRAL
Mono Paiute
Costanoan
Owens Valley Paiute
Monache
Panamint Shoshone
Esselen
Tubatulabal
Salinan
Yokuts
Chemehuevi
Kawaiisu
Vanyume
Chumash
Kitanemuk
Alliklik
Fernandeno
Serrano
Mohave
Gabrieleno
SOUTHERN
Juaneno
Cahuilla
Halchidhoma
Luiseno
Yuma
Degueno
Kamia

0   50   100   150   200 miles

An ethnographic map of California's original civilizations indicates boundaries not greatly different from the modern political divisions. At first thought this may be surprising, but it comes naturally enough from physical and psychological causes: in the west coast's separation from the inland basin area and from the southwest a physical barrier of desert and mountain range confirms differing ways of living and of regarding life. Across the Colorado and Gila rivers to the immediate south and beyond the Smith River northward, cultural influences making these adjacent lands "un-Californian" operate today as they did in the distant yesterdays.

23

A VANISHED GARDEN

Let us look at the land.

In size it is only about one percent of the whole of the continent north of Mexico, but nonetheless it contained and supported more than ten percent of the indigenous population. The stereotype of the miserably housed and fed "Diggers" will not stand up against the actuality. Why, one cannot but wonder, should the claim have been made that a land most generous to its conquerors was niggardly to its native peoples, who understood so well the nature and nurture of its bounty? The Spaniards and Mexicans made no such error, but they were familiar with Mexico itself and with Mediterranean countries whose landscapes and climates suggest those of the west coast of the United States.

And the land, particularly those parts on which the Indians regularly lived, is not impressive or inviting to the uninitiated. A. L. Kroeber writes of it, referring here to the habitat of the Pomo Indians along the Russian River, "The river flows through a series of small enclosed valleys, not a continuous plain. Side streams are numerous, often in deep ravines of some length, yet dry in summer; but springs are abundant to any one familiar with the country. It is typical California land: arid to the eye once the winter rains are over, yellow and grey in tone, but fertile; monotonous in the extreme to the stranger, yet endlessly variegated to those familiar with it and its resources."

Throughout the unpropitious-seeming countryside grew food, medicinal herbs, and roots; materials for clothing, houses, and boats, for utensils and tools; and in it were ample outcroppings of basaltic rock, of flint and of obsidian. Ecologically, the Indians were part of a natural order between whose people and other animal and plant life there was a well-nigh perfect symbiosis. It was a place of unravished forests, streams, valleys, hills, and meadows. The Indians' preservation of the land and its products for the ten thousand or more years of their undisputed occupancy was such that the white invaders wrested from them a garden, not the wilderness it salved their consciences to call it.

That vanished garden cannot now be recreated except in imagination: its climax forests of redwoods, cedars, and pines, its primitive stands of oak trees, are gone. The once untapped and unpolluted creeks and rivers, bays and lakes, are now put to industrial, agricultural, and urban uses. Men with horses, with herds of grazing sheep and cattle, with their axes and plows and finally their bulldozers, have effaced the old contours. The soil profile, once held against rain and wind and the passage of man and four-footed animals by a strong growth of herbal shrubs, scrub, and flowering grasses, is now exposed to erosion and destruction, while the fertile valleys and bottomlands disappear beneath an uncontrolled urban spread. The invaders have altered the face of the land more in one hundred years than the Indians did in ten thousand. Tardily we thrust about trying to save and protect the disappearing wildlife, the native grasses, the trees, the once teeming marshes, the life-bringing bees and birds, even the mountain lion—the natural occupants of brush, stream, marsh, and air, the keepers of the balance—seeing at long last that our land and we will be poor indeed when all these are no more.

[These assertions will bring—have brought—against their authors an accusation of romanticism, of Rousseauesque noble-savage delusion.

Anthropologists are romantics. Without a strong urge to understand a set of values and an esthetic different from his own, no archeologist would undertake the exhausting and time-less task of prodding the resistant earth to give up its secrets, no ethnologist would submit himself to the rigors of learning a strange and unwritten language, of spending weeks, months, perhaps a year or two in total isolation from his own kind, of painstakingly fitting into place, in the final pattern of a culture-whole, the infinitesimal and innumerable items that go into its making. Field archeologists and ethnologists live under conditions that are strenuous and lonely, rugged, sometimes not altogether safe. Anyone who has undergone alone the experience of confrontation of a strange people, who has survived the trauma of culture shock and gone on persisting in his labors, is impelled by an idealism that could not be further from Rousseauian. But the idealism is there and very anthropological it is, a curiosity and a respect for man and his works, wherever and however they manifest themselves.]

Try for a moment to envision the land when it was Indian from Baja California to the Oregon border, how it must have looked as it unrolled before the northward advance of conquistador and padre. There were the sheltered coves, the sunny beaches, the broad shallow rivers emptying into the sea. Inland were the swift creeks and the lush meadows of spring, the smooth valleys rimmed by deeply indented worn-down hills, oak-dotted, the ground covered with a mat growth of grasses, tubers, and clover, green in winter, dry, pale to burnt gold in summer. For freeways and cities and people in fast-moving automobiles substitute a land wholly inhabited by a Stone Age people, without bronze or iron, who made no use of the gold nuggets that were to so inflame the avaricious imagination of the Europeans. Going up and down the narrow meandering trails meant for the feet of men, you would find yourself upon crossing a stream or topping a foothill in another world, where a language was spoken unintelligible to the inhabitants of the world you had just left. There were more than five hundred village-states or tribelets in California, each politically and territorially

A VANISHED GARDEN

A VANISHED GARDEN

independent and constituting separate national entities however small. History has record of one hundred and twenty different languages. There were no doubt more of which no record at all remains, but no one knows how many.

The houses would be of redwood planks, of bark, or earth-covered, clustered in small villages, never alone, never in large numbers, for all Californians were villagers. Kroeber writes, "Adjacent tribes were visited at ceremonies and to some extent wives were purchased from them. Of those next beyond, there was only the dimmest knowledge; and farther, neither rumor nor legend nor interest. At that distance there was only the end of the world or a strange unsighted ocean, and perhaps things that no one wanted to see. . . . A man of substance, wealth or character did not stray or nose about. He remained at home in dignity, or traveled where relatives or old or hereditary friends welcomed him." Everywhere you would find a barefoot, lightly clad copper-colored people: women gathering bulbs and ferns, stringing strips of fish or venison on frames to dry, weaving baskets, sewing rabbit skins together, making a showy cape of mallard and woodpecker feathers; babies in their basket-cradles, small children running naked close to the old men and women sitting in the sun; men stalking rabbits, deer, fishing for salmon, flaking an arrow or spear point, fashioning a bow, a harpoon.

Let us look now at the native Californian: what was his characteristic physique? His temperament? His world view?

THERE WAS A CHARACTERISTIC physical type, with two other types that contrasted with it and with each other: we have pictures that show their considerable differences. Although it is not to be assumed that temperament echoes anatomy and physical traits, it does appear to have done so rather neatly with these people, for each of the three had its peculiarities of build and response and each was different enough one from the other to make the single underlying web of culture particularly interesting.

Between Mount Shasta in the north and Tehachapi Pass in the south and from the crest of the Sierra Nevada west to the sea, lies the heartland of California. Here were to be found most of her Indians, the predominant physical type, and the carriers of the most idiosyncratic culture. Three hundred tribelets of California's five hundred or more belong to this area.

These Indians were midway in the over-all human scale of height and weight; their strong psychological bent was a commitment to a middle way. Their skin was pale copper, burning to bronze under a hot sun. Hair, blue-black and straight. Eyes, black and set wide in the face, with an occasional trace of the Mongolian epicanthic fold. Nose, neither high nor broad; chin, neither jutting nor receding. Teeth, large strong white. Mouth, medium large; lips, neither thick nor extremely thin, overtight not slack. Hands and feet, slender, small. The tendency was to a comfortable corpulence in middle age.*

In almost the exact center of the central area, in the western foothills of the Sierra and on the plains of the San Joaquin Valley, lived the Yokuts

*They were physically strong. A long series of tests made on a dynanometer gives these figures: Indian males from 30 to 50 years of age: 52 kg for the right hand, 49 kg for the left hand; Indian females, same age range, 29 kg for the right hand, 25 kg for the left hand. In similar tests of "Old Americans," that is, Caucasians of at least the third generation in the United States, for the same age range, males registered 42 kg with the right hand and 36 kg with the left hand, whereas for females the figures were 23 kg for the right hand and 19 kg for the left.

HEARTLAND
PEOPLE

HEARTLAND PEOPLE

Indians, a large nationality, who may be taken as the ultimate realization of the heartland people in feature and form, in the extreme rounding of face and body and in a temperament that fitted the ample curves like a second skin. They are to be thought of in the round without angularities of feature or body. Not all Central Indians looked like the Yokuts, as our pictures demonstrate. The Pomo, north of the Yokuts, although as softly molded were of a somewhat different cast. The Yuki, close to the Yokuts geographically, were the shortest Indians in North America. One could multiply the exceptions, but it would still be true that a clear photograph from any one of the Central peoples would not often be mistaken for either a Northerner or a Southerner.

The gestures the people used were undramatic, the fingers somewhat curved, not held tense and rigid. The stance was easy; they stood or sat quietly without fidgeting or restlessness. They were not "built" for speed, that is to say speed was not one of their values. But they could and did walk, dogtrot, and run at a steady easy gait, tirelessly and efficiently, developing this skill as young boys and girls and having it as long as they lived except, of course, in illness or other incapacity. The facial expression was interested—not heavy or dull—but mild. Uncontentiousness and predictability, hence stability, were virtues they believed in and cultivated. Exhibitionism, overdisplay or any behavior that made them conspicuous was thought to be unbecoming and was discouraged.

They were a well-mannered people; early travelers attest to this. To strangers their courtesy was overlaid by a profound shyness which made them formal, watchful, and reserved. Amongst themselves, the strong preference for the underexpressed meant that injuries, troubles, jealousies, hurt feelings, and grudges tended to be "eaten in," not easily forgotten, since nothing in their code and custom provided a natural explosive outgoing reaction. But their reasonableness, their absolute commitment to a middle way, their wish to have good relations were on the whole realized, the physical and psychic strains being for the most part not more than they could handle within their own behavioral values and patterns. There may never have been a gentler or more amiable people.

One looks at a face, memorizes a gesture, observes an action: to report on them will not be too difficult. But to make plain the values that motivate a culture very different from one's own is difficult. Religion, or the law, suggest themselves as starting points, but one knows them to be complex and intermeshing. War would surely be simpler, with its weapons, its mystique, its anecdotes. We shall look first, then, at warfare, letting the gossamer curtain of religion which hangs over all this early world begin to show itself inferentially.

It does so at once, the wholly negative value put upon war by the Californians being a startling revelation of much that was positive in their value system. They did not believe in war: when it came it disrupted the modulated moderate tenor of life in which they believed. In Kroeber's words, "Warfare throughout California was carried on only for revenge, never for plunder or from a desire for distinction." But war never amounted to any clash larger than inter- or intra-family quarrels and village feuds. A death believed to have been caused by sorcery was a common source of a feud (enter religion and law). There were no special weapons as such and when an altercation became a fight, rocks, stones, the hunting bow, and the ever-handy digging stick were used.

Their unwarlikeness was the trait that most downgraded them in the white man's appraisal of the Californians. Here was to be found none of the accouterments or behavior of gallantry, bloodshed, and bravery. No horses, no buffalo, no counting coup on a fallen enemy. No war whoops. No war bonnets. No shields. No armor. No victory orations, no boasting speeches by triumphant braves. If possible the severed head of the enemy or his scalp, in certain circumstances, was taken and sung over in a victory dance, for there was strength to be drawn from a bested foe and the occasion was one for rejoicing in the return to tranquility and harmony. But it was of the utmost religious significance that the body receive proper burial and the soul commitment in good order to the Spirit World. The family and friends of the dead man would risk their lives many times over to recover the body. The numerous Yokuts, the Wintun, Valley Maidu, and Pomo of the Central nations and smaller tribelets among them, and the whole of the Northwest peoples took no scalps at all. Nowhere were scalps kept as trophies, nor did honor accrue to those who took them or dishonor to those who did not. Most of the Indians in California first saw scalping with the Gold Rush.

There were no elaborated victory rituals and no victory paeans to the one who had done the killing; he might or might not meet with the approval even of his own family and village, depending upon what sort of settlement followed the violence and whether relations became better or were worsened by it.

The man who was useful when passions were aroused and blows were being exchanged was allowed no large word in council in normal times. And this was because the Californians observed a true separation of civil and military responsibility by having a dual chieftainship. On those rare

HEARTLAND
PEOPLE

HEARTLAND
PEOPLE

occasions when a feud grew to such a degree of involvement that one village was ranged against another, a leader was chosen to direct the action of the fighting men of his village, the choice falling to one who was known to be brave and skilled in such matters. Responsibility for leadership in normal civil matters was vested in a regular village headman, who was an important and wise and trusted person usually of considerable age, sometimes of great age, a man of substance, of proven stability, usually a wealthy man. His authority, though considerable, rested wholly in the

REASONABLE AND PEACEABLE
ABJURING ALL EXTREMES

ROUND OF BODY
ROUND OF FACE

THEY COULD BE MODELED ONLY IN PLIANT CLAY
NEITHER CARVING NOR CHISELING
WOULD REPRODUCE SUCH ROUNDNESS

THE EXPRESSION CHANGES FROM SERIOUS TO SMILING
WITH THE QUIETNESS OF THE FULL MOON
WHOSE FACE THE YOKUTS FACE INVOKES

12. YOKUTS, Wikchumni subtribe; Wahnomkot, born 1868; photo 1930

13. YOKUTS, Koyeti subtribe; José Vera, born 1868; photo 1935

14. YOKUTS, Chukchansi subtribe; Mary George, age *ca.* 60; photo 1922

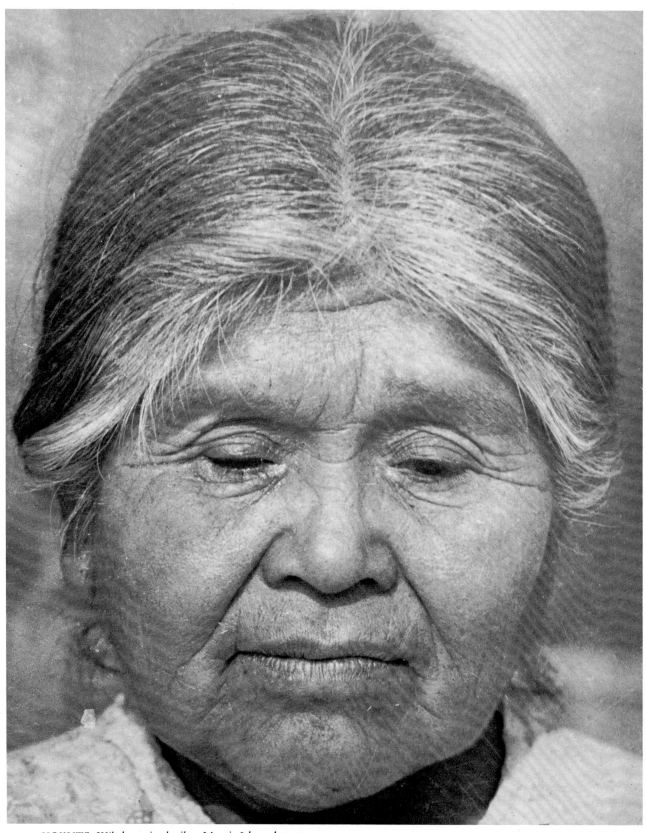

15. YOKUTS, Wikchumni subtribe; Maggie Icho; photo 1939

trust that the people of his village placed in him; he had no power of life and death over any man—he had no power at all except insofar as his people found him to be wise and to have their best interests at heart.

This headman never participated in the fighting or quarreling. This was so even if he was not old and was known to be a good fighter, because, having kept out of the feud, he was able to meet and deal with the equally uninvolved headman of the other village when the time for settlement came. Beyond the headman there was no police force in all of California, nor was there any other governing and controlling body. The subtle rule of taboo and custom, the pressure of village disapproval, with the possibility of banishment by village decision, was the usual discipline. There was no open frontier for the Californian to fade into; over the hill was another nation, another world where a strange tongue was spoken. Nor would that world welcome one who had been banished from his own. Obviously he was a troublemaker and could expect to be sent on his way farther from home, or more probably to be killed if he was considered a threat to neighborly relations and to the peace.

Money-indemnity payment for a death, a bodily injury, or an insult, or other infractions of custom, was universal. Of this law Kroeber says, ". . . it is neither rigid nor ramified. Margin is left for modification according to personality or circumstance or public opinion." It was also more elaborately codified than any other procedure having to do with quarreling or feuding. The headmen were at the center of all indemnity negotiations, whether private or intervillage. Kroeber says, "Money is prized and establishes influence everywhere. . . . It counts for more in public and private life among the average Californian people than among tribes of the Plains or the settled and unsettled tribes of the southwestern United States. . . . Blood money, bride purchase, compensation to the year's mourners before a dance can be held, are institutions known to almost every group."

The money was strings of shells of established length, the shells tubular dentalium and clam discs of a certain minimum size and quality. This money was the usual medium of exchange, purchase, and indemnity. Payments were made under a system of agreed values and customary law.

Life centered in the family house, and in the extended family circle, with the men and older boys spending a good bit of time in the men's house. The men's house was ubiquitous. There the ceremonies appropriate to men only took place: the daily and sacred sweat bath was one such. There they slept, smoked, prayed, and purified themselves before a hunting or fishing trip or before a fight. It was also there they relaxed and talked—

a club house. There the young boy came to receive instruction and initiation. (For the adolescent girl there was a small, separate ceremonial house alongside the family house.)

Children were welcomed, cherished, and treated with gentleness, great affection, and playfulness. Adoption was easy and common, a spontaneous response to a child's need. And this was possible because families were kept small, the population stable and well within the capacity of the land to support it. There is neither archeological evidence nor oral tradition that suggests single or recurrent famine, or fear of it. The tales, some of them, and the prevalence of spring feasts indicate that a severe or a prolonged winter would empty the food storage baskets and there would be some hungry days. The coming of spring and the early run of salmon were celebrated with joy and no doubt with relief.

These people savored life: they liked to eat, to sing, to dance, to make a journey to a nearby village for a celebration and a feast. They laughed and joked, the men alone together in their men's house, the women over their stick games in the family house. They listened as if for the first time while the Old Ones told the stories of ancient heroes and the tales of Coyote whose troubles and tricks old and young found very, very funny even when the story had a moral as it frequently did. (Coyote's role in these stories was much like that of the mischievous talking animals of Aesop's fables and of the East Indian Jataka tales.)

Everywhere in North America shamans were doctors but in California they were more exclusively concerned with the various aspects of disease than they were in other parts of the continent.

Much is made of the more esoteric aspects of a shaman's behavior and powers but it is well to remember that he knew at least as much and probably more than his very well informed patients concerning the properties and uses of all medicinal, poulticing, narcotic, or poisonous plants. He was skilled also in setting bones and in treating sprains, torn ligaments, and other injuries or wounds. The theory of the cause and cure of disease determined much of his procedure for treating a physiological illness or a psychosomatic one. Illness was caused by a "pain," often in the form of a tiny arrow, that had been shot somewhere into the body, and, to cure it, the pain must first be located and then sucked out: only a shaman could do this. At this point we are in religion as well as medicine, for a shaman would have undergone long and arduous training, would have been in touch with a "guardian-spirit"—the supernatural spirit from whom he learned his skill. Only certain people were competent to be shamans for they must be able to go into trance and to function in trance. A good shaman was exhausted at the end of a curing session; he was successful in locating the pain and in sucking it out (else he did not stay long in practice), and the hands that went searching, searching over the patient's body, gently feeling, prodding at significant spots, were knowledgeable hands. Through aptitude, interest, and long application, he knew much about illnesses.

There was some specialization among shamans; some were diagnosticians only; others, curers or "suckers." There were also snake shamans who specialized in curing snake bite. And there were weather shamans and bear shamans; the weather shamans undertook to make rain and the bear shamans took on themselves certain aspects of a bear, some were thought actually to turn into bears, and so to become strong and useful in doing away with monsters and other enemies.

The shaman's power was great and he might be greatly feared: he might use his knowledge and power to evil ends, even to implanting a disease in someone. A shaman who lost too many patients might expect to be killed once enough people were aroused and suspicious. It was a highly paid as well as a demanding and dangerous profession requiring a person of a certain determination, competence, and caliber to undertake the training in the first place and to maintain the integrity and generate the charisma needed for a useful and rewarded career. The shaman, however much leeway he was given in what was believed properly to belong to the practice of his profession, was subject to the prevailing legal code. A death for which he was responsible, or believed to be, was usually punished by death. He must make compensation for lesser injury. If people lost faith in him, or if he began to feud and compete with another shaman, he would certainly lose, if not his life, his practice and his standing in his own community— and as in other dilemmas in a small-world system, there was no place to go.

Legal and religious sanctions meshed in all sorts of ways for each person. What one must do and what one must not do in life's crises and what were the meanings and place of these crises, were matters spelled out, objectified, as were the rules and directions for everyday living. Precedence covered procedure, but not in a legalistic, mundane way, for all precedent came from an Other World, a superhuman origin and authority going back to the beginning of the world and to the Creator God or Gods: religion pervaded and determined the whole of life.

The foundation of religion was in the Creation. In the accounts of it were the making of the world itself, its animals and the first people. Were there ever a more truly Chosen People than these small tribelets of Cali-

HEARTLAND
PEOPLE

fornia? Each occupied a world specially created, with its own people, language, and Way, by benign Creator Gods and Heroes. All was accounted for, planned and made for them. All had existed before there were people, through the providence of a prehuman and superhuman race whose devotion was such that they gave up their world to its human inheritors. These predecessors of men were still about, under the earth or in the Sky World or across the ocean or here on earth in self-transmuted animal or natural-object form and still concerned with men. One or another of them would come to a vision-seeking man if he dreamt well and was sufficiently pure and dedicated. Dreams were an intrinsic part of life, both ordinary dreams and vision-sought power dreams. And dreams led to the Great Ones—the earlier inhabitors and establishers of things-as-they-are. From dreaming came shamanistic power and other power and all knowledge.

One is never told quite fully why these Great Ones chose to resign their earthly paradise to man. The accounts usually allege that it was at the insistence of some one of the more powerful of them, usually the principal creator. They seem to have felt they must go but with freedom to choose their place of retreat, or to stay, having changed into something harmless like a butterfly, a little lizard, a spring, a seastack. Their era invokes not a golden age but something more intimate, sunnier, greener, lighter in tone, gentler and gayer, a place inhabited with intercommunicating higher and lower gods and adventurous heroes and great numbers of clever, talking animals and birds and insects. The happiness of creating the world, the sadness of departure, and the continuing concern with the affairs of their lost world carried over to the people who came after them. They inherited, as it were, the old brooding nostalgic love of the land, of the Way as it was anciently set. And this determined the direction, the force, and the temper of their religious understanding and practice and emotion, hence their values and what they would and would not do and be.

The earth hears you.
The sky and the sacred mountain see you.
If you will believe this you will grow old.
And you will see your sons and daughters
And you will counsel them in this manner
When you reach your old age.

—Said to boys in Luiseño initiation ceremony

FROM WHAT WE KNOW of them, the coastal Indians were closely akin to those inland whom we have been describing, but, except in
the north, it was they who first and principally came under Mission
and Spanish control—we know tantalizingly little of them. It has become
the practice for the Bureau of Indian Affairs and popular writers to refer to
the tribes south of Los Angeles as the Mission Indians, and for that reason
we use the term even though it covers a dozen separate aboriginal nations.

Archeological remains of the Chumash Indians of Santa Barbara and
Father Geronimo Boscana's excellent account of the Indians attached to
Mission San Juan Capistrano make it amply evident that they, along with
all those Indians who are identified now by names of missions, possessed a
more varied and richer culture than that of the inlanders. Some of them
were the Gabrieleño of the Los Angeles area, the Nicoleño and others of
the off-shore islands, the Luiseño in the vicinity of Mount San Jacinto,
and finally the Diegueño of San Diego.

These erased cultures and peoples were in themselves varied and in certain of their features bore indubitable mark of an ancient, it is to be
guessed, two-way flow between them and the Pueblo Indians of the Southwest. Moving east from them to the Cupeño around Warner's ranch (Agua
Caliente) and the Cahuilla of the Colorado Desert-Salton Sea region, we
cross a cultural bridge that carries us way from the heartland–west-coast
cultures to the Colorado River and its Yuman peoples, who were themselves distinctive and special and who suggest cultural-historical possibilities lying beyond—in Baja California, in Mexico.

We should here remind the reader that by "heartland" we mean the
unadulterated, peak expression of a people and its culture. We do not
mean its most colorful or varied expression. It is a fact that it is among the
simplest of the heartland people of California that the dynamic of their
Indian Way is perhaps most readily discovered and understood: nothing
stands between its religious ethical and moral motivations and their simple
statement and performance. All Indian California is based on this stark
foundation. But, moving out from it as we are now doing, we feel the old
grief that so great a loss of ceremonial and esoteric riches was suffered

SOUTHERN
MISSION TRIBES

when the "Mission" Indians and their culture succumbed. Theirs was an enrichment on what we have been describing from the inland Central people, of which we have only fragmentary highlights: ground paintings of different styles—some cosmological and esoteric, others literal maps of the sky and earth; an elaborated lunar-solar calendar system; a chieftainship sometimes hereditary; a socially stratified society; pantheons of gods original as something out of the old Greek world.

Among these Mission Indians there was the most concentrated development, probably the center, of the "toloache" cult, that is to say, of the cult built around the vision-producing jimson weed or datura plant. At the

16. LUISENO, Saboba Reservation; photo 1897

heart of this cult was the prolonged agony of initiation of the boy into full manhood. In all it covered many weeks of fasting, of physical and mental ordeal, of learning a new view of the world received through the violent mystic experience with which the initiation was begun. The young initiate was given to drink an infusion made from the root of the datura plant. The narcotization from this drink was extreme; occasionally a boy died from it. The physical effects lasted for days; the dream-visions the boy received under influence of the drug determined his mystic thought for the rest of his life. We are here at the extreme point of the mystic-tending religious bent of the Californians, and of their elaboration of the initiation cult.

SOUTHERN
MISSION TRIBES

17. DEGUEÑO; Manuel Lechuza; photo 1902

COLORADO RIVER PEOPLE

OUT IN THE DESERT, past the Cupeño and Cahuilla, one might expect to find a people who were intermediaries and transmitters of the toloache cult between the Southwest and the far west coast. But not so. To be sure, datura grows plentifully on their desert land; they have always known its dream-inducing properties. But the cults surrounding it were to the west, the east, and probably to the south of them. They eschewed its use altogether, along with its cult and indeed all cults, nor did they feel any necessity for an agonizing initiation of their boys and girls into manhood and womanhood. We are on the Colorado River and with the Mohave and other Yuman peoples of that river.

With the Yumans we are describing for the first time Indians who were far enough out of the way to escape the annihilating brunt of invasion, who live today where they have always lived, and whose numbers have remained large enough for them to keep their identity. They move into participation in the surrounding white culture with far less of the terrible disadvantagement that most Indians experience. They are more than a remnant people; the white population along the river and in the desert is light today as it has always been.

The Yumans have kept much of the "real" look because there are still among them their Old Ones to take the young to the sacred mountain and river sites, to repeat to them the old epic tales of their people, and to teach them to dream. Life—much of the old life—was being lived along the river when Kroeber went there at the opening of this century, and new epics were still being dreamed when he went back in 1953 as they no doubt are today. The inner life survives—despite the damming of the river, despite the threat to the canyon to the north, which their own God Mastamho created and into which he put the river, and despite the threat to the great fruitful delta of the river. (Is not that delta the largest truck garden in the world?)

Anciently, as today, the Yumans lived along the river below the great defile of Eldorado Canyon, above which is the gorge that culminates in the Grand Canyon, and downriver all the way to the mouth. They were beyond

42

the protective screen of the Sierra Nevada but were in contact with the sea.

Of the river Kroeber says, "This enormous Nile, flowing through narrow bottom lands bordered sharply by sandy stretches, high mesa rims, and barren mountains rising on both sides from an utterly arid desert, provides a setting wholly unlike any heretofore encountered. And [its] civilization is equally distinct . . . the stream course is a furrow that separates Arizona from California; and whoever lived in the trench belonged as much and as little to one area as to the other."

The Yumans were the only Californians to engage in agriculture, and theirs was only partial. They dropped their corn and squash seeds into the red ooze left by the retreating flood waters of the river, but then gave the seeds little heed, letting them sprout and grow as they would with sun and rain, with only occasional help from the planters in the way of weeding and cultivating. Their technique was adequate, given the unusual garden conditions, but casual, with little resemblance to the Zuni and Hopi Indians to the east of them who were true agriculturists. Nor were the planted crops the Yumans' only foods; they shared the California food pattern of hunting, fishing, and gathering edible wild plants.

These riverine people were taller than other Californians; in fact they were the tallest North American Indians, and larger boned and heavier built. They were, nonetheless, more Californian than foreign, their generous features remaining contoured and rounded and the expression benign. Kroeber says of them, "Their carriage is loose, slouching at times and rapid at others. They lack the graceful dignity of the Pueblo Indian and the sedate stateliness of the Plains warrior, but are imposing to look at. In walking, they are apt to stoop and drag, but break readily into an easy trot in which they travel interminably. The women . . . carry themselves very erect and with a pleasantly free and easy gait." He goes on to further characterize the Yumans as "noticeably more responsive and energetic than other Indians of California. They are rarely sullen. The California trick of eating in a grievance is foreign to them . . . they are frank, inquisitive and inclined to be confiding. . . . The demeanour of the men in repose has a certain reserve . . . but they unbend readily, talk volubly, and laugh freely. Jokes are greeted uproariously. All ages and both sexes demonstrate their feelings openly. Young men may be seen walking with their arms around each other, fathers kiss their children irrespective of who is about, girls in love manifest their sentiment in every action. There is something very winning in the instantaneousness of the generous Mohave smile."

The Colorado River people occupied a larger country than that of any

COLORADO RIVER
PEOPLE

COLORADO RIVER PEOPLE

of the Central tribes and were the only ones with an unprotected flank, exposed to harassment from the nomadic Apaches beyond the river, who preyed also on the Pueblos. This meant that they must protect their eastern borders or be overrun. They were more warlike than other Californians, having long since become tough defenders of their land and willy-nilly the protectors of those peacefully living peoples to the west, who might otherwise have had hungry and aggressive Apaches intruding upon their very private little worlds.

They had even developed a most effective weapon, a short club shaped like an old-fashioned potato masher, which they used in hand-to-hand combat, bringing it up with a short motion to smash the enemy's face. They were also among the few Californians to practice scalping. They did not look for trouble, but if they wanted to travel or to hunt, they did not hesitate to leave the river and to risk a fair certainty of confrontation of an enemy.

The Yuman over-all view, encompassing as it must their stretch of river and bordering desert, was wider than that of the heartland peoples, for whom the village was the true unit of social and political organization. The Yumans, too, had their villages and village identification, but they thought of themselves as national entities, and among themselves they freely crossed tribal boundaries. They were natural geographers, with a deep interest in the landscape and an accurate sense for both position and distance. The Mohaves are the most numerous of the four surviving Yuman nations, and in 1952 and 1953 Kroeber traveled by car through Mohave country in the company of an old Mohave man. Together they went to many of the places named in a Mohave song cycle and epic account. Kroeber could locate many of the places on a modern geodetic survey map, especially if the place was a spring, a hollow, a hill, or other physical feature. He found that the distances traveled each day according to the story worked out realistically on the ground, as did the locations of the overnight stopping places or special spots for singing a long series of songs. This is the more interesting because the story had been recounted to Kroeber in 1906 and for the further remarkable fact that it had, the whole of it, been dreamed in the first place by its teller over a period of many years.

The Colorado River people were less shy than other Californians, less reluctant to make acquaintance with peoples and cultures differing from their own. They were cosmopolites of sorts who lived to travel, visiting all parts of their own country and going beyond it deeper into California. (To the east would be enemies.) Kroeber tells of groups of Mohave who traveled as far as the Chumash of Santa Barbara and the Yokuts of the San Joaquin Valley: "Sheer curiosity was their main motive, for the Mohave were little interested in trade . . . timidity did not discourage them and they were as eager to know the manners of other people as they were careful to hold aloof from adopting them. . . ."

Women occupied a more nearly free and equal position in Yuman society than elsewhere: premarital sexual experience was not especially encouraged but carried none of the stigma that attached to it elsewhere; a woman, like a man, could divorce if she so wished, again without stigma; a woman was given more voice generally and, perhaps because of the occasional wars and the great interest in traveling about, the wife and mother took more responsibility and was given more authority than in a more tightly living group.

Yuman shamanism differed from that of the Central people in that, besides the usual doctoring function, their shaman could cause the soul of a man to leave his body and to be lost. He could, as well, search out a lost soul and return it to its body. Thus a shaman was watched with some suspicion and engaged with caution, for with such control over the soul he could cause a man's death—a man cannot long survive the loss of his soul. And he could save a man's life. All this was accomplished by dreaming, for it was these same large, relaxed, and comfortable Yumans, these practical geographers and travelers, who, when it came to the inner world and its mystique, found in dreams and dreaming a richer, a more benign and pervasive substance than did any other California people. Even as they allowed themselves a larger outer world, they committed themselves to a more intense inner world—they too found balance, a middle way. Kroeber writes, "The direct [Yuman] basis of all religion, tradition, ritual song, and shamanistic power is individual dreaming. . . . An autobiographical statement by one of their shamans reveals this attitude. . . . *Before I was born I would sometimes steal out of my mother's womb while she was sleeping, but it was dark and I did not go far. Every good Doctor . . . begins to understand before he is born.* Every narrator is convinced that he was present at the ancient events he tells of. If the Yumans were to express themselves in our abstract terminology, they would probably say that the phenomena of dreams have an absolute reality but that they exist in a dimension in which there is no time and in which there is no distinction between spiritual and material."

Beginning with life in the womb, dreams permeated the whole of a man's days to his death. And there was continuity between the earlier and the later dreams. They were additive, like a story told in installments; they were cumulative, their impact and power building as dream was added to

COLORADO RIVER PEOPLE

dream. A great doctor was one whose dreaming had at last completed his knowledge and skill, over many years of dreaming. In their literature, particularly in their long prose epics, the teller would be an old man who had, throughout a long life, dreamed a "new" story, dream by dream, episode by linked episode: it would be old and familiar in most of its parts but its songs and happenings would differ from earlier epics. And, so much at home were they in their fused world of dream and nondream, they threw away all aids to dreaming. They needed neither drug nor dance nor cult nor costume nor formula recitation to induce their dream to come to them. Why the distraction of ritual and initiation and drink when you need only sit or lie, quietly turning the sun of your thoughts inward where the dream lay waiting, the dream you began in your mother's womb and had been

RELAXED AND FULL OF CURIOSITY
DREAM ORIENTED

THERE IS A LARGENESS IN THESE PEOPLE
IN THEIR BODIES
IN THEIR IMAGINATION

GEOGRAPHERS OF THE FAR BORDERS OF THEIR LAND
GEOGRAPHERS OF THE FAR BORDERS OF
CONSCIOUSNESS

THE SMILE COMES EASILY   GENEROUS
THE MAN'S SMILE AND THE WOMAN'S SMILE

18. MOHAVE; Minnie Moos; photo 1908

19. MOHAVE; photo before 1900

48

20. YUMA; Chief Miguel; photo *ca.* 1900

*You know how some men are quick and strong and know the things to do, how people like
to do things for them, and how they have a gift for getting everybody cheerful? Well, those
men were* kwoxot—*tribal leaders.*   —A Yuma Indian's remarks about chiefs

COLORADO RIVER PEOPLE

elaborating ever since? You need only will yourself into your dreams to be once again in a place and a life already well known to you where you mingled with ancestors and gods of the most distant past. When you returned from the dream you would bring with you a new chapter, newly dreamed by you, to add to the epic story of your people.

It is not too much to say that the whole of the Yuman sensibility was contained and found expression within their dream world, whether the mundane or the religious.

21. MOHAVE; Jack Jones (Indian name Kwaknialka); photo 1908

ALONG THE MOST northerly coastal shore and the Klamath and Trinity rivers of northwest California were a quite different people from the Yuman. These were the Yurok, Karok, and Hupa, and below them to the south and east eight or more further nationalities who shared many of the culture traits of the three, diffusing more and more with distance into the typical Central culture.

The Northerners resembled the Central majority in the median size but in nothing else could they be called median. Handsome, without being tall they gave the effect of height, being slender and long-limbed. The nose was high-bridged, not large, not beaked, a knife edge; mouth firm but graciously molded; skin light with red showing in the cheeks; eyes having somewhat more of the "almond" contour than elsewhere in California. Some Japanese are reminiscent of them in their features, in the relatively pale skin and reddish cheeks and in a nose bridge that is the highest in the Orient.

These people shared in a culture that extended from Alaska to the mouth of the Klamath River—the Northwest Coast—but they lacked much that was characteristic of the people to the north of them and participated in the over-all culture of the California heartland. They stood out from the Central peoples, not so much in the few material objects they alone had, nor in certain of their customs that differed (although these were distinctive as shall be seen), but rather in a temperamental tension which gave their practices greater definition even to exaggeration. We confine ourselves to a brief paraphrase of highlights from Kroeber's account of them, with which he opens the *Handbook* and from which it is tempting to quote at length, for no people intrigued him more than they. Read "Yurok" to mean Yurok-Karok-Hupa, all three being meant, as they looked alike and were identical culturally except for speaking separate languages.

They shared none of the Northwest Coast delight in war, warfare meaning to them what it meant to the Central people: they made no distinction between war and murder, and their so-called wars were really feuds. There was more feuding and contention along the Klamath than farther south,

YUROK-KAROK-
HUPA

YUROK-KAROK-HUPA

the Yurok being a proud and money-minded and legalistic people to an extreme degree found nowhere else. They sometimes used a stone-headed mallet when the fighting got rough and they sometimes wore a chest and body protector of elk hide or of wooden rods woven together with strings of fur or bast. And here alone the women might take a hand, coming to the aid of their men if they were getting the worst of a fight. (Not so with the Mohave women. They hated fighting and the punitive expeditions their men went out on; they saw no sense in them and they were not slow to say so).

The Yurok took no scalps and did not decapitate a foe. They held no victory dance or other celebration; instead they held a "settlement" dance when the bickerings and disagreements over the amounts of the indemnities each side must pay had been agreed upon; all damage to people and property must be paid for. A wealthy and prominent man paid more than a poor and obscure man, and, in private feuds as well as one involving many people, the victor or victors paid higher than the vanquished: *noblesse oblige*. They must be said to have been fairly preoccupied with the accumulation of wealth, with success and status. In Kroeber's words, "The Mohave adhere to a belief in dreams as the basis of everything in life with an insistence equaled only by the Yurok devotion to the pursuit of wealth." Theirs was an aristocratic ideal: it was necessary to be wealthy in order fully to realize and express their wholly individuated mode of manners, character, bearing, and behavior. They were both elegant and puritanical.

Individual rights always took precedence over communal ones. For example, a performance of the essential World Renewal rites could not take place until whoever was in mourning had been paid indemnity for "violation" of his grief and status as mourner. The logic of the Yurok view was that since the ceremony was desirable, nay essential, to the well-being of all, it was the responsibility of those engaging in it to satisfy whatever personal claims stood in the way. In Kroeber's words, "To us the legal sanctioning of the obtrusion of a private interest in the face of a general need seems monstrous. This is anarchy. But the Yuroks were an anarchic people."

The legal principle of money payment obtained all over California, but the Yurok alone, says Kroeber, "measure the precise value of every man's life or wife or grief. Every injury, each privilege or wrong or trespass is calculated and compensated. . . ." But a little farther along he says, "The Yurok is wholly Californian in his lack of any visible symbolism to give expression to the economic values which are so fundamental with him.

He is without crests or carvings or totem; he has no seating in order of rank, no names and fixed privileges or priority. His society follows the aims of the North Pacific Coast with the mechanism of the societies of California. . . . Property and rights pertain to the realm of the individual and the Yurok recognizes no public claim and the existence of no community." It was the individual or the individual household that controlled—in effect, owned—hunting and fishing rights on particular stretches of coast or stream or country and rights to a particular stand of acorn oaks or timber. Many Yurok feuds were over trespass of these rights.

To go back now to the dance performed upon the settlement of a feud, each party to the feud brought a basket containing indemnity payment and around his basket each party danced and sang, a stone's throw apart. A priest pronounced the proper formula over each basket, after which the contents were distributed as agreed, and then they all danced together, this time in a single line abreast, singing songs accompanied with drum and flute—lively and triumphant songs. There was the risk that new fighting might break out, feelings so recently having run high, but this did not usually happen, not because the feelings were assuaged but because each man knew he must control them, proper payment having been made.

A custom of the Yurok otherwise unknown in California was that of keeping slaves—not many and always their own people. Never mistreated, they were part of the household and extended family; they worked only as did others and were cared for. Slavery arose usually from debt and often a man asked to become his debtor's slave. It may have been a less onerous solution than to be an independent but poor person with a burden of debt, for his status was already of the lowest and as a slave he was at least attached to one or another of the wealthy households. The institution was a curious remnant-influence from the Northwest Coast.

The Yurok had no trace of the ceremonial and competitive giving away of wealth, called the potlatch, of the Northwest. To be wealthy meant that you paid the full bride-purchase for your wife as would your sons and that these women could be chosen from the best families anywhere up and down stream and would be virgins of impeccable rectitude and chasteness. It meant that you owned a home well built, well situated, and with a name of its own; and that within were well-filled chests of treasure.

Treasure consisted first of all in many strings of shell money, but prestige treasure was a complete dance regalia for one or more of the traditional dance-feasts. Very old and beautiful were the white deerskins, woodpecker headdresses, and giant obsidian ceremonial blades which the dancers wore or carried. Owning them meant your wealth was such that you could

YUROK-KAROK-HUPA

announce yourself the host for a dance and could feast the many who came
for as long as they chose to stay. A successful feast and dance might go on
twenty days or more. It meant that you would, when your daughters came
to marry, demand and receive a top bride-price for them and that they
would have been much sought after. You were respected and looked up to
as one of the most aristocratic householders on the river and with equal
discretion, prayer, and industry your sons were in a position to continue
your line among the wealthiest and best families.

Yurok religion differed in several respects, notably in its shamanism,
from that of the Central peoples. Yurok doctors, with extremely rare
exceptions, were women—all their great doctors were women. (See the
picture of Fanny Flounder, page 150, one of the greatest Yurok doctors,
and, so far as we know, the last.) The Yurok doctor differed also in that
her power came, not from a guardian and supernatural spirit, but from the
spirit of an ancestor, who had usually also been a doctor in her time.
Another and greater difference was that Yurok doctors kept their "pains"
inside themselves although these same pains would be fatal to anyone else.
Also, no malevolent use of their power was made by the Yurok doctor,
nor was such use feared. There were in the community other people who
exercised power for mischief or to do real harm, but they were usually men
and were known as poisoners.

A Yurok girl gave evidence, usually before puberty, of qualities that
would make her a doctor. Such a girl was rarely allowed to continue her
serene and sheltered role in her home. Older doctors would seek her out,
beginning her training and cultivating the sensibilities as well as the
strength required in the arduous role of healer and diagnostician. Going
into trance and being able to function in trance were two of the necessary
skills. (When she had become professionally established there was no
barrier to her marrying and having children and other woman-life experience and she usually did so.) But while still in her early adulthood she
would receive in a dream-trance a first gift from her "donor," of a pain,
perhaps only a small one. She might be in long trance with this first pain,
or quite out of her usual senses. And the pain made her sick. The other
doctors and the priests—men in charge of rites and ceremonies—took her
into the men's house where they kept her awake and dancing and watched
her very carefully. Left to herself at this crucial time she would have died
or gone mad: the pain controlled her. Gradually her dancing became less
frenetic, and at last she was able to swallow the pain, to bring it up into her
hand, to dance with it, to let it flutter above her head and to call it back
into herself: she controlled the pain. As she grew in age and skill she

acquired stronger pains in later dreams—the more pains she controlled, the better and wealthier a doctor she would be.

A doctor was required to accept all patients who wished her to treat them. The agreed payment, which depended upon the wealth and social prominence of the family, was made in advance; if the doctor failed to effect a cure she returned the whole sum to the patient or his family. It was suspected that there were some unscrupulous doctors who, while sucking out a major pain and thus curing the patient, would meanwhile plant a little one in its place so that there would be reason for the return of the patient for further treatment. But the Yurok motive was greed, not malice. A doctor did not try to kill a patient nor did she come under suspicion of having done so, even when the patient died while under her care.

The religious ceremonies distinctive of the Yurok were the World Renewal rites, held in the autumn and in the spring, several each year. Their esoteric part consisted in long formulaic recitations by a priest. They were in dialogue form, as between a human questioner and the Wogé Spirit of the particular place. (Yurok called the prehuman inhabitors of the earth the Wogé. They even knew something of their language, certain of the formulas and prayers being in "Wogé.") The dialogue was, you might say, an exchange on a rather high level with explanations from the priest and assurances from the Wogé as to the continuing good state of the world and, at the Wogé's request, a gift to him of tobacco or some herb. At the end, the priest threw angelica root and tobacco on the fire as an incense offering. The rites took place at specified and historic spots along the Klamath River in a given sequence, as the Wogé had themselves ordained. They were to insure bountiful wild crops, abundance of salmon and deer, and to prevent earthquakes, stars from falling, illness, hunger, floods, and the destruction of the world. It was a joyous occasion with singing and dancing and feasting for many days. People traveled up or down river and from the farthest reaches on the coast to attend it.

It was Kroeber's conclusion that this peculiar and specialized civilization attained a higher level than others in California, not in its religion especially, but "in an achieved classic clarity." The imagination and execution were clean and incisive whether on the conceptual, philosophic plane or in handicraft, where the hand-adzed redwood plank house replaced the simpler pole and brush or earth-covered house and the preference was for bone and horn over wood in fine tools and utensils. Where river travel—even ocean travel—was in the heavy but graceful redwood dugout canoe instead of wooden or balsa raft. Such preferences, which took in the more

YUROK-KAROK-
HUPA

YUROK-KAROK-HUPA

laborious physical materials and psychic exercises, bespoke an esthetic regard to be found again with the far-away and only archeologically known Chumash of Santa Barbara. And finally Kroeber says, "Yurok mythology is woven in strange colors. Stirring plot is slighted. . . . A lyric, almost elegiac emotion suffuses it. Affection, homesickness, pity, love of one's natal spot, insatiable longing for wealth, grief [of the Wogé] at having to leave the world they so loved. . . . Tales that will interest a child or please a naïve stranger of another civilization do not appeal to the Yurok, who have developed refinedly special tastes in nearly everything with which they concern themselves."

These people in the northwest corner of the state suffered almost mortally during the Gold Rush—more than did the Colorado River people, but less, far less, than those interior Indians who were athwart its direct path. The canyon of the Klamath River is deep and steep, a protection to its people and a deterrent to a prospector. Nor were these northern and coastal riverine Indians ever dislodged from their homeland; those who are alive today live where their ancestors lived. They were never herded onto a reservation, never suffered the immolation of anonymity.

Today, ethnologists and linguists making the acquaintance of their descendants discover a certain late bloom of the old ways. The Indians

SENSITIVE PURITANICAL
AND PERFECTIONIST

ONLY THE FINE STROKES OF THE CHISEL
COULD GIVE THE FACE SUCH DEFINITION

THE BUILD SUGGESTS DELICACY WITH STRENGTH
IN REPOSE, A POISED TENSION

TO THEIR GESTURES AND BEARING THERE CLINGS
FROM THE OLD PROUD DAYS SOMETHING ELEGANT
ARISTOCRATIC

22. KAROK; photo 1907

23. YUROK; Mrs. Ira Henry; photo 1910

24. YUROK; Alice Frank Spott; photo 1907

YUROK-KAROK-HUPA

may be Christians; their ethic remains Yurok, nor do they deny the old gods. They are tougher than other Indians in their legal battles with the whites, bringing to them their old familiarity and skill in law and litigation and having an instinct for selecting good outside legal advice and aid. They will fight to the last redwood, to the last king salmon to save from destruction and pollution the still incomparable woods and streams of their land.

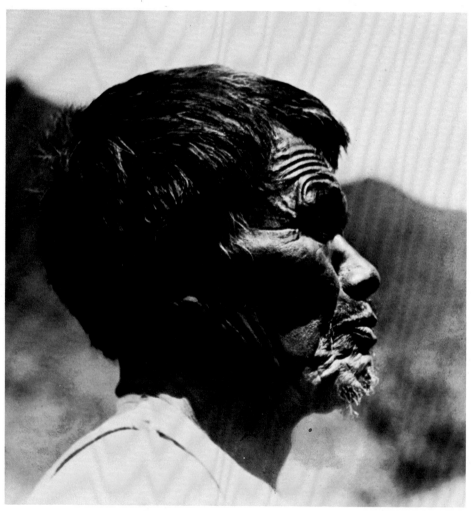

25. YUROK; Umits, born 1844; photo 1907

II FOLLOWERS OF THE WAY

It is winter in a village on the sunny side of a stream in the hills and it is evening. A curl of blue smoke comes from the smoke-hole of an earth-covered house. Inside, supper is eaten, the baskets washed and set to dry, the children and their parents and the old ones sit close together, quiet, warm in the house pit in a circle around a log fire, listening to Mother's Brother who is telling of the time before the world was created.

STORY OF CREATION

In the beginning there was no land, no light, only darkness and the vast waters of Outer Ocean where Earth-Maker and Great-Grandfather were afloat in their canoe. Earth-Maker cast a long line into the water and brought up from the bottom of the ocean a pat of earth no larger than his hand. He placed it on the surface of the sea where it drifted on the waves. Then he stretched his arms, fingers open, toward the piece of drifting earth and it grew and spread and thickened until it became the World.

Earth-Maker and Great-Grandfather beached their canoe on the shore of the new-made world and walked from end to end, for it was flat and empty. As they walked they thought and thought of all they must do before people could live there. While they thought and spoke together, they reached their arms, fingers extended to the North, the East, the South, the West, to the Above and to the Below. In this way they caused mountains and hills and valleys to form where there had been only flatness, and creeks and rivers to flow and cut through the land to the sea. They called Sun and Moon to come to light the World.

They planted the seeds of acorn oaks, of fruit trees, of berry bushes and grasses, which sprouted and sent roots deep into the ground.

They put deer and elk and bear and small four-footers to live in the hills and open valleys; low-flying birds in the trees and brush; high-flying birds to go back and forth between the earth and the Sky World; and salmon and eels and the lesser fish to swim up rivers and into creeks.

When the world was finished and complete, Earth-Maker took soft clay and formed the figure of a man and of a woman, then many men and women, which he dried in the sun and into which he breathed life: they were the First People.

He gave homes to them, some in a fold of the hills, others by the sea. To each he said, "Here is your home and the home of the children who will be born to you. Your land reaches from here to here." So saying he indicated a place upstream and one downstream, also the crest of the first line of hills and perhaps a tall pine or a boulder or other marker to show the boundaries beyond which the land belonged to someone else.

Then Earth-Maker and Great-Grandfather taught the First People to hunt and fish, to make fire, to build houses and to fashion tools. They taught them also the tongue which each should speak, its songs and ritual words; the taboos to be observed for each age and each special event in a man's and a woman's life and all the rules of customary belief that go to make the Way.

When Earth-Maker and Great-Grandfather saw that the First People had learned and understood all these matters, their task was finished. Sadly, because they loved the world they had made, they said farewell and went underground forever. Since that time, since the beginning, the descendants of those First People, even to us here in this house, continue to live in the place where the Ancestors lived, to speak the old tongue, to keep the taboos, and in all matters to follow the Way.

YOUNG ONES

26. MOHAVE; photo *ca.* 1900

27. YOKUTS, Chukchansi subtribe; Nellie Graham; photo 1922

28. MONO PAIUTE

Sleep! Sleep!
In the Land of Dreams
Find your Grown-up Self
Your future family.
Sleep! Sleep!
        —Wintu Song

65

29. CAHUILLA

Bird Song   *Daybreak people are chirping*
Above me on the roof
Alighting they chirp tci-tci.

—Wintu Song

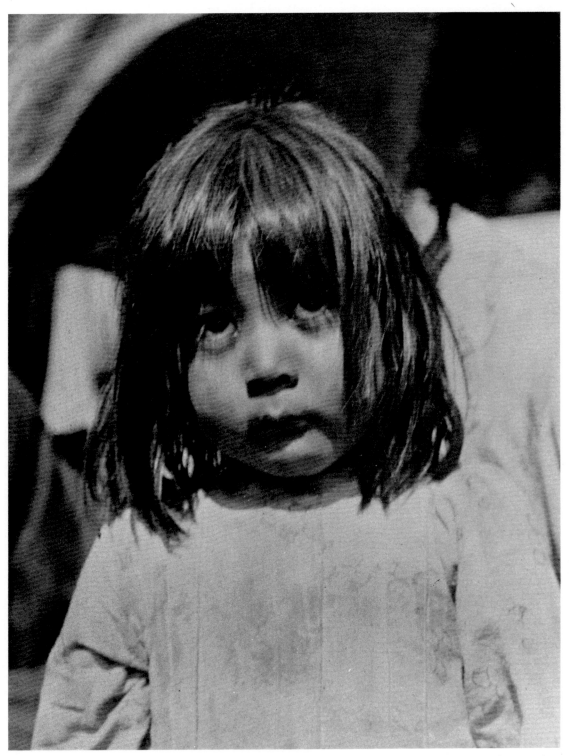

30. MOHAVE; photo 1908

YOUNG ONES

31. MOHAVE; photo 1907

In the beginning the world was rock. Every year the rains came and fell on the rock and washed off a little; this made earth. By-and-by plants grew on the earth and their leaves fell and made more earth. Then pine trees grew and their needles and cones fell every year and with the other leaves and bark made more earth and covered more of the rock.

If you look closely at the ground in the woods you will see how the top is leaves and bark and pine needles and cones, and how a little below the top these are matted together, and a little deeper are rotting and breaking up into earth. This is the way the world grew—and it is growing still.

—Northern Miwok Creation Myth

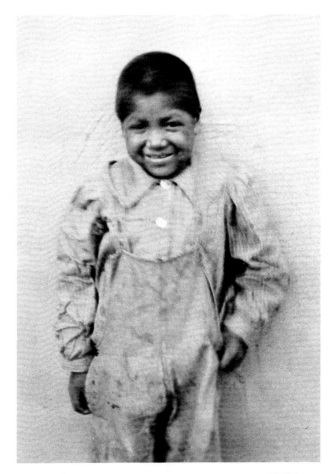

33. YUMA

32. YOKUTS

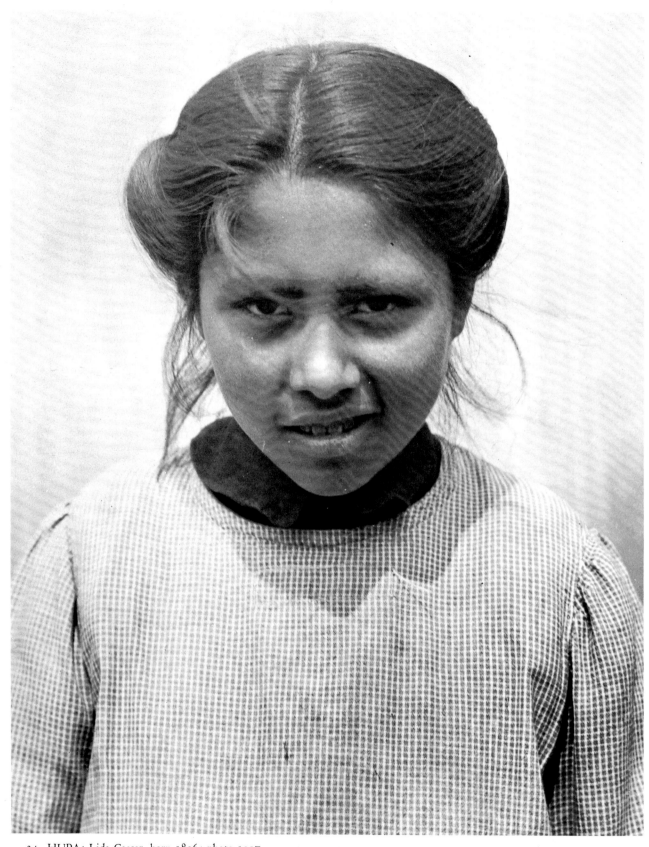

34. HUPA; Lida Caesar, born 1896; photo 1907

35. MOHAVE

YOUNG ONES

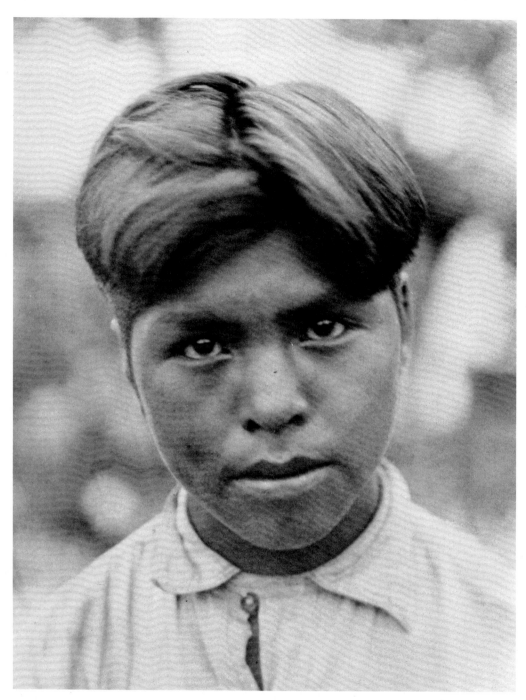

36. YOKUTS, Gashowu subtribe; William Wesley; photo 1922

37. MIWOK, Yosemite Valley; Cozy; photo 1910

38. HUPA; W. Smoker and H. Campbell; born *ca.* 1895; photo 1907

39. MOHAVE

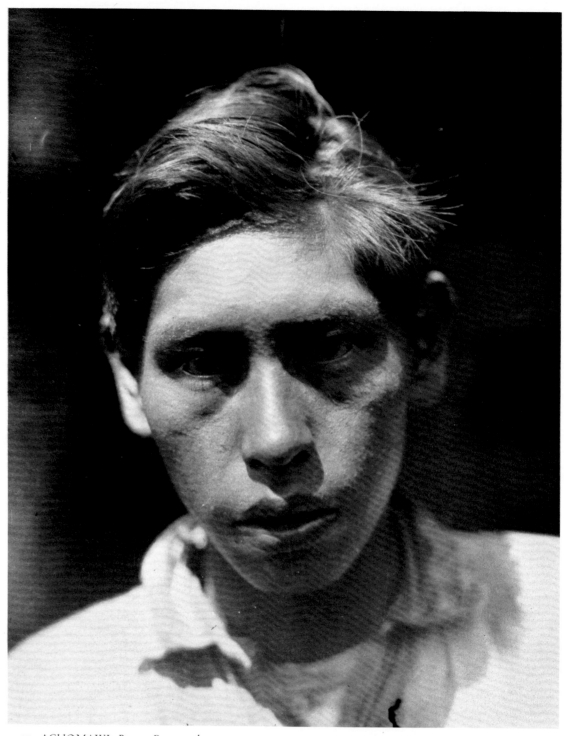

40. ACHOMAWI; Barney Ronur; photo 1922

GROWING UP

The growing boy went to sleep in the men's house at night and to spend his days with an uncle or a father and with the older boys, learning a man's world.

He went on quests for visions, seeking supernatural aid that he might become a strong hunter or a wise doctor.

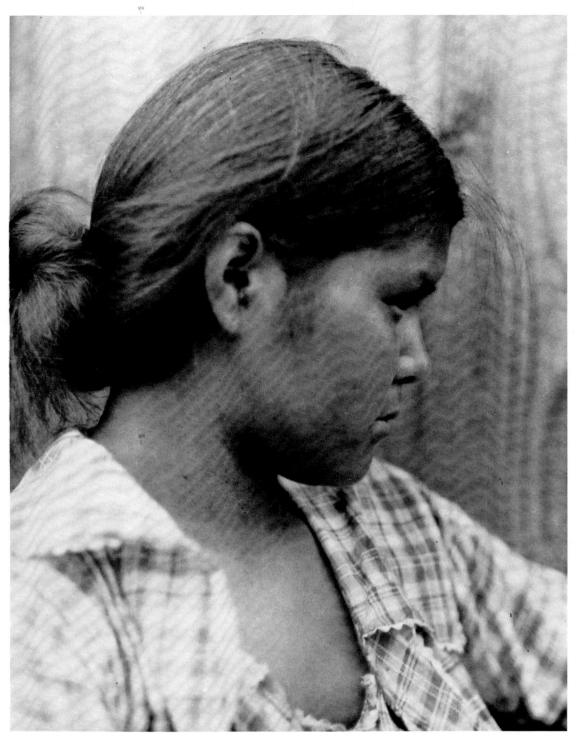

41. MONACHE; Annie Anderson, born 1902; photo 1922

The girl stayed in the big house with the women except for certain nights and days she spent in lonely vigil in a small house of her own.

She was taught a rigid woman's code by her mother or an aunt or a grandmother and she learned the many onerous tasks, the skills, the patience and endurance and strength she must have to become a desirable wife and a good mother.

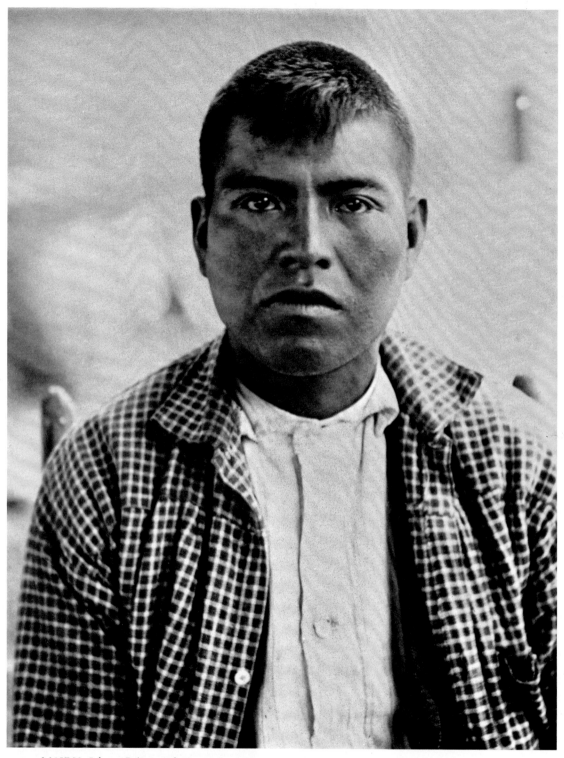

42. MAIDU; Johnny Paiyute; photo 1900

Said Elder Uncle, speaking to his young nephews:

See these old men and women: they paid attention to this counsel which is of grown-up people, and they have already reached old age.

One must respect his elders, listen to them, give them food freely; not eat meals secretly, refrain from anger, be cordial and polite to one's relatives-in-law. Then one will be stout, warm, and long-haired, will grow old in good health and have children to whom to pass on counsel, be talked of when death comes, and have one's spirit go to the sky to live.

43. MOHAVE

Said Elder Uncle, speaking to his young nieces:

You must not look sideways, must not receive a person in your house with anger. You will welcome your relatives-in-law when they arrive at your house. At some future time you will go to their house and they are going to welcome you politely. Pay attention to this speech and as your son or daughter grows up, you will bathe in water, and your hair will grow long and you will not feel cold, and you will be fat. Do not neglect to paint yourself, and people will see, and you will grow old, and you will see your sons and daughters.

79

44. HUPA; Gladys Matilten; photo 1907

45. MOHAVE; Paul; photo 1908

46. WINTUN; Mrs. Ray Wilson, born 1898; photo 1922

47. MOHAVE

48. ATSUGEWI; Hattie Brown, born 1907; photo 1922

It is above that you and I shall go
Along the Milky Way you and I shall go
Along the Flower Trail you and I shall go
Picking flowers on our way you and I shall go.

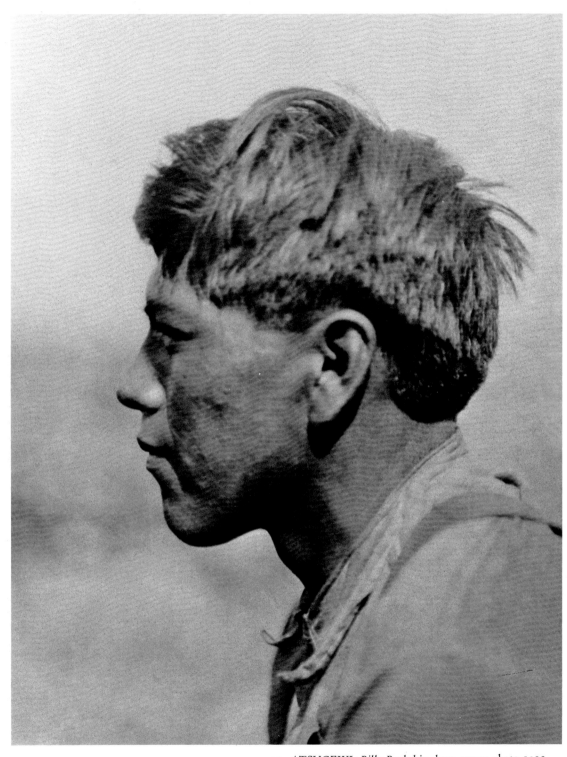

49. ATSUGEWI; Billy Buckskin, born 1900; photo 1922

Where will you and I sleep?
At the down-turned jagged rim
Of the sky
You and I will sleep.

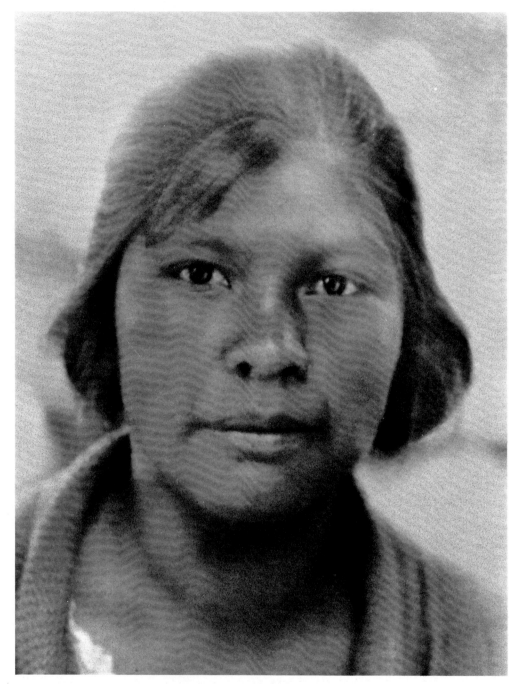

50. WASHO; Dorothy Washo, born 1892; photo 1922

51. MOHAVE; Leslie Wilbur; photo 1908

52. CHEMEHUEVI

53. CAHUILLA

YOUNG ONES

54. KATO

THEY HAD NO METAL and were without the wheel. They had no horses nor any beast of burden. The dog was their single domesticated animal.

They were fishermen, hunters, and gatherers, fashioning their tools and utensils, clothes and ornaments suitably to their purposes and to be pleasing as well to hand as to eye: delicate spoons of horn; steatite pipes; beads of seeds and shells, stone and bone; deerskin skirts, fringed and hung with abalone shell pendants; feather headbands; fur and feather blankets; obsidian and flint knives, scrapers, rasps.

They were makers of baskets: waterproof cooking baskets; serving baskets small enough to fit a child's hand; ceremonial baskets elaborately patterned and embellished with feathers and tiny pendants of shell; and great storage baskets made of pine roots, almost as high as a man, which when filled took a strong man to lift or carry.

What did they find to eat and to fill their huge storage baskets? They ate acorns, venison and lesser game, salmon and smaller fish. For those who dwelt by the sea there were the myriad variety of salt-water fish and shellfish; they ate eel, which appealed to the Indian palate as it did to the ancient Roman.

There were elk and bear but lone hunters did not seek contest with them. There were rabbits and squirrels, raccoons, badgers; and porcupine, if you were unarmed and weak, in need of an easy kill. The flesh of reptiles or amphibians was not eaten, but the larvae of insects and fresh-water mussels were considered delicacies. Small birds were netted, and quail, in fine nooses—and ducks and geese and all waterfowl.

They were traders: olivella, dentalium, and abalone shells were passed inland from the coastal people across one tribal boundary and then another until they reached the people of the hills.

Obsidian, flint, salt, furs, and special wood for pipes and bows moved out of the hills into the valleys.

Acorns, grown in the broad central valleys, found their way farther inland, and westward to the coast.

But the people moved only within the boundaries of their own world in response to salmon runs, deer migrations, the succession of ripening crops and ceremonies, a seasonal flow back and forth.

A MAN'S WORLD
AND A
WOMAN'S WORLD

A MAN'S WORLD

Nuts and berries and other fruits, seeds, tubers, and greens ripened and resowed themselves unaided and unattended. Some of the harvest—animal, fish, and vegetable—was eaten fresh in season and the rest was dried on racks and frames and stored against winter needs.

The women knew where to go to gather medicinal herbs and roots to heal stomach complaints and headaches, to staunch bleeding and to poultice wounds. They knew the contraceptive and abortive plants, those that induce vomiting and those that bring on dreams and visions. And they knew where the sacred tobacco grew.

Gathering in the wild crops, fishing, hunting, trailing the deer, nutting, and acorn gathering, this rhythm learned from nature was interwoven with the human drama of living.

Each event was marked by dance, song, feast, taboo, ritual.

With the recurrently changing moons the time came round again for a
World Renewal ceremony—
Thanksgiving Feast to mark the harvest—
Dances and prayers to prevent or to cure illnesses—
Ritual mourning processions in memory of the dead—

Such the diurnal, seasonal, round of California's wholly encompassable world.

THE HUNTERS
THE STRONG ONES
GOOD WITH BOW AND SPEAR
WITH HARPOON
AND SLING

WHEN HE WAS A BOY
THE HUNTER WENT ALONE INTO THE HILLS
FASTING FOR MANY DAYS AND NIGHTS TOGETHER
PRAYING FOR STRENGTH AND SKILL
THAT HE MIGHT BECOME A GREAT HUNTER.

55. MODOC; Ollie Hardy, Sam Riddle, Bidwell Riddle; born *ca.* 1892; photo 1907

56. MAIDU; Johnny Bob, born 1880; photo 1900

57. BANKALACHI; Dan Williams, age 62; photo 1935

58. MOHAVE

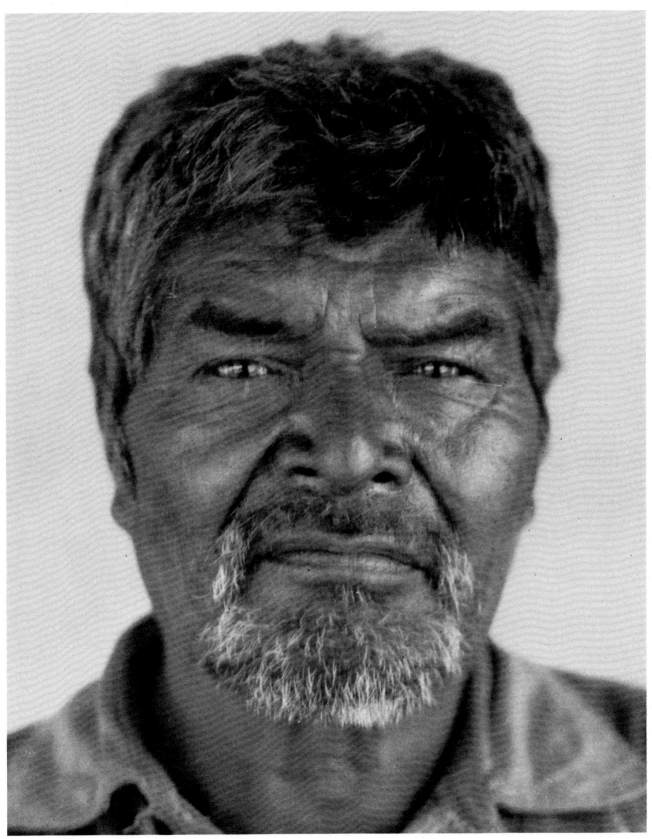

59. MIWOK; Sam Casoose Domingo; photo 1922

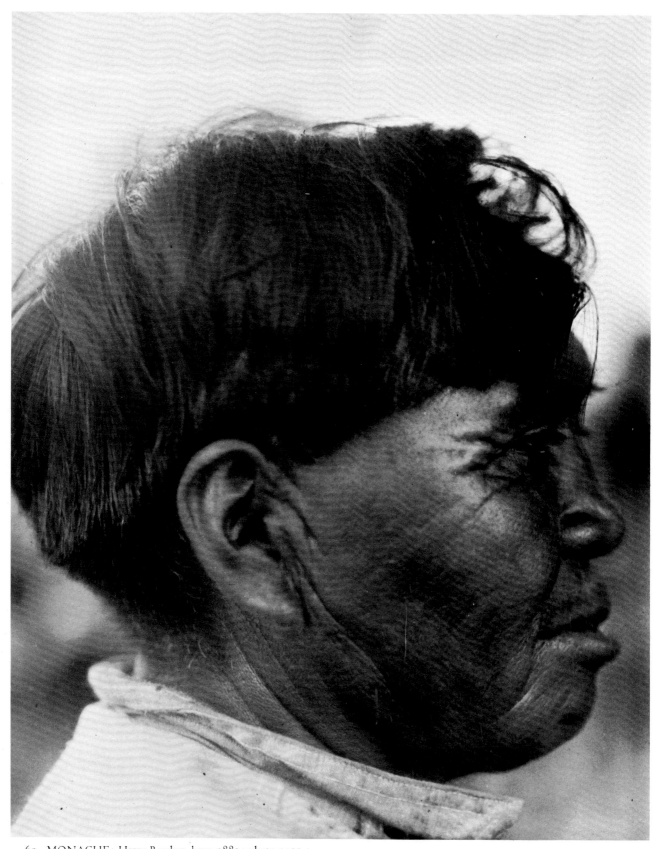

60. MONACHE; Harry Beecher, born 1882; photo 1922

61. HUPA; Captain John, born 1837; photo 1901

When they first came along with a pack-train, we ran away and hid. They came up to the flat and went around among the houses of the village. They began to buy manzanita flour with small blue beads. Those with brave hearts traded with them. Some of us ran away from them. The babies were hid in the storage baskets.

—Coming of the white man as told in 1901
by a Hupa, born *ca.* 1827. The incident
described occurred *ca.* 1832-1837.

62. POMO; Pummuke, born 1834, died 1906; photo 1903

63. MOHAVE; Bluebird; photo 1908

64. MAIDU; Lawson Anderson, born 1860; photo 1900

65. HUPA; Baldy, born 1837; photo 1907

A WOMAN'S
WORLD

THE GATHERERS
THE PICKERS
THE ROOT DIGGERS
THE ACORN-MUSH MAKERS
THE STORERS
THE BASKET WEAVERS

THE WIVES
THE MOTHERS

66. COAST MIWOK; wife of Chief Huyumhayum; photo 1905

67. MONACHE, Holkoma subtribe; Mrs. Ben Hancock; photo 1903

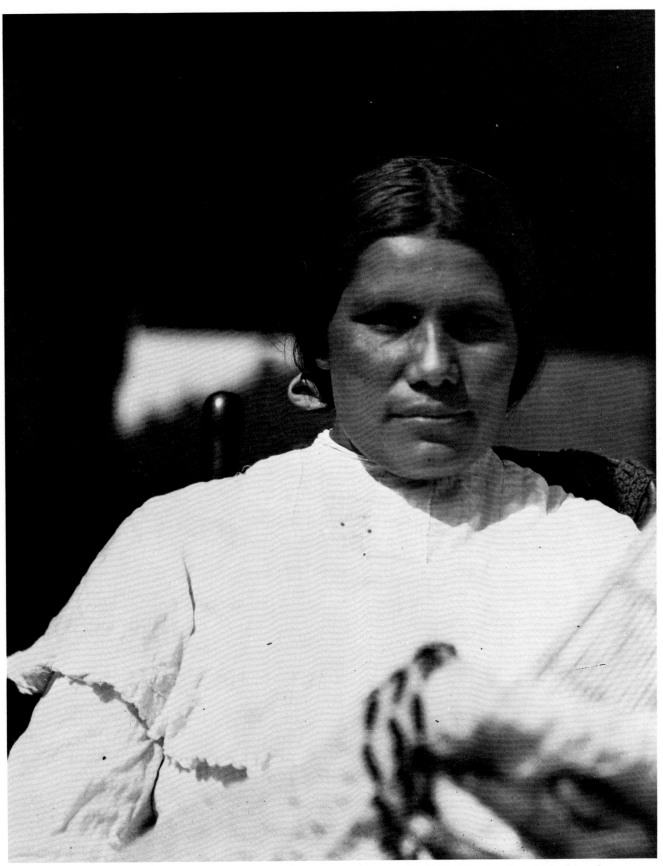

68. HUPA; Lucinda Jack, born 1879; photo 1907

69. PANAMINT SHOSHONE; photo 1931

70. YOKUTS, Chukchansi subtribe

Walowtah the Cloud Maiden, sang:

This will be the last song
Of our people, the First People
In this, the First World.

People, now we are going.
For you it will be hard
You faultfinders and fighters.

But I am not sorry
The First World is passing.
People of the next world
Will not be long in coming.

It is for them my song is sung.
I watched the making of this world
I shall see the coming of the next.
I shall be proud.

As a bird I shall sail through the sky.
Now I am Walowtah, the Cloud Maiden.
Soon I shall be Lowechah, the Eagle.
I shall be proud.

—from *Annikadel*, C. HART MERRIAM

71. MIWOK; Sally Ann; photo 1910

72. MOHAVE; photo 1908

73. YUROK; Molly, born 1847; photo 1907

74. MONACHE; Wiunu, born 1820; photo 1918

Wiunu told the story of her life in 1915, when she was about ninety-five.

She admitted to being a restless person. During her long life Wiunu could recall moving twenty-three times, three or four times because a close relative had died and she had not wished to remain in the village where the death had occurred, but mostly she had moved, she said, "just to be moving."

She lived less than five years on the average in any one village, yet the map of her changing residences shows not only that she never crossed the border of her own Mono world, but also that she satisfied her restlessness within an area of no more than sixty-eight square miles.

MAN AND WIFE TOGETHER

    MANY MOONS
    WINTER MOONS
    SUMMER MOONS
    COME AND COME AGAIN

75. WINTU; Wintun Joe and wife; photo 1903   115

76. MAIDU, Nisenan subtribe;
Chief Hunchup (born *ca.* 1832) and wife; photo 1904

77. MOHAVE

78. YOKUTS, Chukchansi subtribe; photo 1902

79. MOHAVE; photo 1908

80. MIWOK, Chowchilla subtribe; photo 1903

81. MONACHE; Chief Chepah, his wife, son, and daughter-in-law; photo 1902

OLD ONES

THE OLD ONES
FULL OF YEARS

THE WISE ONES
THE STORYTELLERS
THE TEACHERS

THE ALMOST
ANCESTORS

82. WAILAKI

123

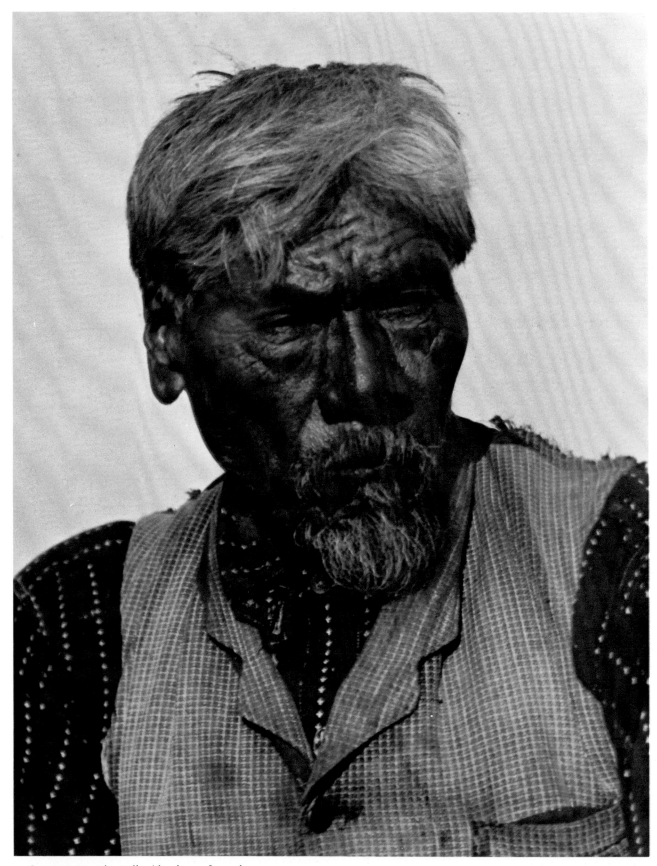

83. POMO; John Fullweider, born 1842; photo 1907

84. MONACHE; Annie Antone, born 1862; photo 1922

85. POMO, Habenako subtribe; Chicken Seagull, born 1852; photo 1907

86. HUPA; Chicken Hawk, born 1837; photo 1907

87. MONACHE; Watcuwate, born 1842; photo 1922

From the east
He came west
Against the mountains.

Flowers he picked just now
Flowers from my grave
Flowers he picked just now.
—Wintu Song

PROTECTED, PEACEFUL, UNCOMPETITIVE, provincial, and settled, the Californian gave full play to the mystic contemplative will, passive but powerful, which characterized the American Indian psyche and temperament. Nowhere was this more apparent than in religion.

Dreaming was intrinsic to the religious understanding. They all dreamt. Beyond the recollective dreams that roil to the surface of consciousness from the sludge of the primitive unconscious, they willed themselves to dream, positive, life-enlarging dreams. The dreamer went sometimes on a fabulous dream-journey, but more often he succeeded in summoning to himself the spirit of a Hero, a Creator-God, or an authoritative Bird or Animal or Fish who spoke to him as it had spoken in the days before men were put on the earth. The Spirit could be expected, having come, to make the dreamer-petitioner a personal gift of knowledge or skill or power with instructions for its use and increase.

The Indian introverted and mystic-tending systems were not of the Christian-mystic sort. Kroeber says, "Though their world is full of deities and spirits, these are approached by the avenue of magic, by the performance of an action which they [the gods] will like and which will compel their aid, rather than by any direct communication as of person to person." The formula recitation is not like a Christian prayer; it lacks all intimacy as between suppliant and his God. Its intent is to compel to oneself something of the mana, the magic power that belongs to the supernatural; the force of the formula resides within its form whose words and word arrangement create this force. Formulas and vision-quests are similar to the sacrifice by which the ancient Greek propitiated his gods. The blowing of tobacco in the several sacred directions, the burning of aromatic herbs, and the leaving of food in the grave, all of which the Indians did, are sacrificial and propitiatory acts. The will of the gods to which man is bound as a part of nature prevailed. The spirit world and the world of

THE AVENUE OF MAGIC

THE AVENUE
OF MAGIC

living man were of equal reality and inherence. Death was a part of life. To the west lay the Land of the Dead. There, when a person died, his spirit journeyed to remain forever with the ancestors, with the other dead, in joy and plenty.

All explanation of natural and unnatural phenomena was locked in myth, fixed, unchanging, predictable. An earthquake happened because a giant, who slept beneath the earth's surface, rolled over in his sleep. An eclipse of the sun, the Pomos knew, meant that one of the Sky Monsters was at his old trick of trying to devour it. They lost no time in blowing up a fearful din, even to beating their dogs to make them howl, and thus frightening the Monster into disgorging the sun (or moon). The Yurok World Renewal rite was calculated to prevent disaster. The logic of mythic belief is of equal validity with scientific belief: no eclipse has ever been permanent; overwhelming natural disaster never, in all its thousands of years, came to the Yurok world.

Recalled piecemeal, mythic explanations may seem merely quaint— folklore, fairytale. But in their place they never float free, casual, unrelated. Even the most exhaustive and meticulous recordings of the oral learning of any preliterate people is partial, out of context, and suffers from the double distortion of translation into a strange tongue and into a world view exotic and unsympathetic to it. There is something awesome in trying to conceive the whole body of myth, held in oral memory from generation to generation, for myth then is seen to encompass history and science, philosophy and literature.

A quality of the mythic ambiance of the Californian was its wholeness: a rational accounting of the natural world and ethics and belief were interwoven, a single fabric. He was saved the schism between science on the one hand and morality, ethics, and belief on the other, whereas modern man's mythic underpinnings, now largely subconscious, tend to fragment his psyche.

They were small worlds, those of the California Indians, which appear at a distance more static, more unvarying than they were to those living within them. Inward turning, boundaried, stable, the life within was enriched by the importance of the intimately known and infinitely beloved— the personal, the ritual, the seasonal—and by the always unforeseen event that is part of the simplest world, however confined and coherent and monotonous.

Our own appetite for the new, stimulating, extroverted, and everchanging comes from an orientation foreign to the Californian habit and preference. A story heard a hundred times and known by heart was appreciated for its familiarity and for its infinitesimal variation as one story-teller told it or as another, for the associations it set going in the long memory of the listener. The familiar was also the comforting, the supporting, the reassuring.

It could scarcely have occurred to a Californian to ask who he was, to question his own identity, being perfectly identified to himself, his family, friends, village, and tribelet, secure in his place, in his present, in his future even unto and beyond death. The Way was known and was known to be good.

Progress in our meaning would not have been part of the thinking within such traditional and conservative cultures as California's. Change, slow change, there was: a new migration pushed a valley tribelet into the foothills; a small valley changed ownership because one group became large enough to absorb the whole of it; languages evolved, a dialect becoming a language no longer recognizable as related to the older root form. A woman added a new motif to the design she was weaving into a basket; a man altered somewhat the form or added to the function of the elkhorn tool he was fashioning. A philosopher conceived of a high god; an artist-astronomer made a ground painting showing the sky world with more vision than any had before him. Tales from over the hill were brought home from a feast and became part of the literature; a song or dance of a neighboring people was memorized and adopted. Life, as it does everywhere, evolved, because no two persons behave wholly alike. Each word uttered, each act performed, each reaction registered, introduces change, but with paleontological slowness.

We today are inclined to be impatient of slowness, of the repetitive-nesses in life. But . . . who is to be sure that a traditional culture does not more richly repay the human animal with health, serenity, sanity, and inner strength than does one that changes its values with each generation, that multiplies the choices, the possibilities, and ultimately the decisions to such complexity and inconsistency that personal identity, right and wrong —the Way—become dim and amorphous and are lost.

History, as we said earlier, is in part the succession of peoples. The face of man mirrors his own history and the world he has known, its physical and its psychic aspects.

You are looking at the faces of people some of whom were old enough when they saw their first white man to remember that fateful occasion.

It is our hope that, looking, you may read in those faces something, even if only a little, of their world, their way—something of the life and death of a people.

THE AVENUE OF MAGIC

When Red Cane [the white man] comes
We Wintu forget our songs.
                    —from a Wintu Song

REMNANT PEOPLE

CLOTHES FOREIGN TO BODY AND HABIT

PERVASIVE DISCOURAGEMENT
LOSS OF PURPOSE
POVERTY
NEGLECT AND
RESIGNATION

THESE THE BITTER FRUITS OF
INVASION AND
CONQUEST

Down west
Down west we dance.
We spirits dance
We spirits weeping dance.
                    —Wintu Song

88. MOHAVE

89. YUROK; Stone, born 1835; photo 1907

90. HUPA; photo 1903

135

91. MIWOK; photo 1913

92. GABRIELINO; photo *ca.* 1900

93. HUPA; photo 1903

94. YUROK; Kaheah; photo *ca.* 1910

95. YUROK; Henry Campbell, born 1853; photo 1907

96. YOKUTS

97. MAIDU; Bill Brooks, born 1830; photo 1900

98. YUROK; Mrs. Childs, born *ca.* 1810; photo *ca.* 1910

KEEPERS OF THE WAY

ON THESE FACES
APPEARS THE SIGNATURE OF STRENGTH
OF SPIRIT THAT HAS TRANSCENDED SUFFERING
OF FORCE OF CHARACTER
OF FAITH PERSISTING DESPITE TRAGEDY AND RUIN
OF THE OLD, THE REAL, LOOK
SECURE, COMELY, SERENE, HUMANE

99. WAPPO

100. MIWOK; Lena Brown; photo *ca.* 1910

101. MOHAVE

102. POMO

103. HUPA; photo 1903

104. MOHAVE

149

105. YUROK; Fanny Flounder, born 1870

Fanny Flounder, the last and one of the great Yurok Doctors.

From the verandah of her redwood house which was built high up on a sea-facing bluff, Fanny looked down almost vertically to the mouth of the Klamath River, and there one day she watched the ocean break through the bar which the river had built up. Fanny shook her head.

You see what happens. The earth tips so far that the ocean spills into the river. Whales will come up the river!

And all this is because there are no longer enough Yurok people left.

When there were many of my people they danced and sang stamping their feet hard on the earth.

This kept the earth from tipping and the ocean from flowing into the river.

Fanny Flounder of Espeu tells how she became a doctor.

I had been dancing for power during several summers. At last I dreamed that I was at the horizon's edge where the dome of the Sky World, rising and falling gently, touches the waters of Outer Ocean, making the waves which break on the shores of our own flat world. From the rim of the sky, blood dripped and hung like red icicles. The Spirit of a doctor stood beside me. She reached up as the sky edge lifted, picked off one of the icicles of blood and saying, "Here, take this," she put it in my mouth. It was icy cold.

Then I knew nothing more. When I came to my senses, much time had passed and I was lying in the wash of the breakers at Espeu. Several men were holding me—I was out of my mind. They took me into the sweathouse, carrying me all the way because my feet turned under me as if there were no bones in them. The men took turns carrying me on their backs and dancing.

After five days of dancing in the sweathouse I was resting and I felt a craving for crabmeat. One of the doctors brought me a crab claw but the first bite I took made me sick. The doctor said to me, "Let it come, let it come!" . . . It came, and with it came the telogel, the pain. Then everybody in Espeu came to the sweathouse and sang while I danced. I was strong as soon as the telogel was out of my body. The doctor said, "Stretch out your hands reaching for the telogel." I did that and the pain flew back into me.

This pain is of blood. When I hold it in my hands you can see the blood drip between my fingers. It is my strongest pain. The song I sing when I suck out blood says, "When the sky moves up and down you are traveling in the air."

106. MOHAVE; Ashpram; photo 1908

107. MOHAVE; photo before 1900

108. MONACHE; Jack Littlefield; photo 1922

109. MIWOK; Sophie Thompson, born 1868; photo 1923

110. MIWOK; Captain Eph; photo 1903

111. YUMA

112. JUANENO, of Mission San Juan Capistrano; Chola Martina; photo 1907

113. MOHAVE; Bluebird; photo 1908

KEEPERS
OF THE WAY

Robert Spott was born in Weitspus, his father of the house Wôgwu, his mother of the house Sohtu. His parents saw to it that he received a thorough Yurok education, and he attended the Hoopa Indian Government school. Robert Spott fought and was gassed in the First World War. A citation from the French government for an act of personal bravery was found among his things after his death; he had never mentioned it. He was co-author, with Alfred Kroeber, of "Yurok Narratives," 1942.

Robert is endowed with an excellent memory, his natural inclinations are intellectual, and above all he is possessed of extraordinary sensitivity to the value of his native culture. He knows as much of the old Yurok ways and beliefs as the men of his father's and grandfather's generation, and is infinitely better able to communicate them through his ability to organize ideas and to make standards articulate. The details have remained in his mind because they are the flesh and blood of a system in which his personality lives, though of necessity increasingly in recollection and feeling, instead of overt behavior, but without serious impairment of these inner affects: nostalgia was an outstanding quality of the old Yurok life, so that Robert's dwelling in the sentiment of the past has not warped his picture of it.

—ALFRED LOUIS KROEBER

114. YUROK; Robert Frank Spott, born 1888

115. MOHAVE

The Creator is finishing the world. He sings:

Darkness will go down in the west
Light will come up in the east.

Sounds will come from the air
Clouds will come on the water.

Fresno Co., July 1922; Lowie Museum negative 6827.

61. HUPA; Captain John, born 1837; photo P. E. Goddard, 1901; Lowie Museum negative 3062.

62. POMO; Pummuke, born ca. 1834, died 1906; photo C. Hart Merriam at Stoney Ford, Colusa Co., June 1903; Lowie Museum negative 23213.

63. MOHAVE; Bluebird; photo A. L. Kroeber, 1908; Lowie Museum negative 4314.

64. MAIDU; Lawson Anderson, born 1860; photo R. B. Dixon, 1900; American Museum of Natural History negative 12556.

65. HUPA; Baldy; born 1837; photo A. L. Kroeber, 1907; Lowie Museum negative 3720.

66. COAST MIWOK; wife of Chief Huyumhayum; photo C. Hart Merriam, 1905; Lowie Museum negative 23214.

67. MONACHE, Holkoma subtribe; Mrs. Ben Hancock; photo C. Hart Merriam, Sycamore Creek, north of Kings River, 1903; Lowie Museum negative 23215.

68. HUPA; Lucinda Jack, born 1879; photo A. L. Kroeber, 1907; Lowie Museum negative 3725.

69. PANAMINT SHOSHONE; photo C. Hart Merriam at Olancha, Inyo Co., April 1931; Lowie Museum negative 23216.

70. YOKUTS, Chukchansi subtribe; photo E. S. Curtis; Southwest Museum print 4010-A.

71. MIWOK; Sally Ann, daughter of Chief Dick; photo C. Hart Merriam, Aug. 1910, Yosemite Valley; Lowie Museum negative 23217.

72. MOHAVE; photo A. L. Kroeber, near Needles, 1908; Lowie Museum negative 4326.

73. YUROK; Molly, born 1847; photo A. L. Kroeber at Kepel, Klamath River, 1907; Lowie Museum negative 3821.

74. MONACHE; Wiunu, born ca. 1820; photo E. W. Gifford, Aug. 1918; Lowie Museum negative 6189.

75. WINTU; Wintun Joe and wife; photo C. Hart Merriam, July 1903; Lowie Museum negative 23218.

76. MAIDU, Nisenan subtribe; Chief Hunchup, born ca. 1832; photo C. Hart Merriam, near Auburn, Placer Co., Dec. 1904; Lowie Museum negative 23219.

77. MOHAVE; photo C. F. Lummis; Southwest Museum collection.

78. YOKUTS, Chukchansi subtribe; old woman who was taken to Mission San Juan Bautista when young, and her three daughters; photo C. Hart Merriam at San Juan Bautista Mission Sept. 1902; Lowie Museum negative 23220.

79. MOHAVE; photo A. L. Kroeber near Needles 1908; Lowie Museum negative 4332.

80. MIWOK, Chowchilla subtribe; mother, daughter, and grandchildren; photo C. Hart Merriam near Mariposa, Mariposa Co., 1903; Lowie Museum negative 23221.

81. MONACHE; Chief Chepah, his wife, son, and daughter-in-law; photo C. Hart Merriam at Northfork, Madera Co., 1902; Lowie Museum negative 23222.

82. WAILAKI; photo E. S. Curtis, Southwest Museum collection.

83. POMO; John Fullweider, born 1842; photo S. A. Barrett, Lowie Museum negative 3870.

84. MONACHE; Annie Antone, born 1862; photo E. W. Gifford, July 1922; Lowie Museum negative 6833.

85. POMO, Habenako subtribe; Chicken Seagull, born 1852; photo S. A. Barrett at Round Valley Reservation, Mendocino Co., 1907; Lowie Museum negative 3953.

86. HUPA; Chicken Hawk, born 1837; photo A. L. Kroeber, 1907; Lowie Museum negative 3650.

87. MONACHE; Watcuwate, born 1842; photo E. W. Gifford, July 1922; Lowie Museum negative 6829.

88. MOHAVE; Southwest Museum collection.

89. YUROK; Stone, born ca. 1835; this old man, who never learned to speak English, provided ethnologists (in 1902 and 1907) with the very lengthy letter-perfect memorized ritual formulas which had to be given before the first salmon of the season could be taken at the mouth of the Klamath River; this ancient oral literature has been published in "World Renewal," by A. L. Kroeber and E. W. Gifford, University of California Anthropological Records, Vol. 13, No. 1, 1949. "Stone" is derived from one of his several Indian names, Stun. He was otherwise known as K'e-segwa akwetl, whose meaning is "father from the house named Segwe'u in the village of Katimin." Lowie Museum negative 3795.

90. HUPA; photo P. E. Goddard, 1903; Lowie Museum negative 3039.

91. MIWOK; photo E. W. Gifford in Amador County, July 1913; Lowie Museum negative 5574.

92. GABRIELINO; photo G. Wharton James, ca. 1900; Southwest Museum collection.

93. HUPA; photo P. E. Goddard, 1903, at Blocksburg, Humboldt Co.; Lowie Museum negative 3034.

94. YUROK; Kaheah, at Weitchpec, at confluence of Trinity and Klamath rivers; photo A. W. Ericson ca. 1910; he stands on stone platform in front of sweathouse; Lowie Museum print collection.

95. YUROK; Henry Campbell, born 1853; photo A. L. Kroeber, 1907, on Klamath River below Weitchpec; Lowie Museum negative 3812.

96. YOKUTS; Southwest Museum collection print 3805.

97. MAIDU; Bill Brooks, born 1830; photo R. B. Dixon, 1900; American Museum of Natural History negative 12377.

98. YUROK; Mrs. Childs, born ca. 1810; photo A. W. Ericson, ca. 1910 at Trinidad Bay, Humboldt Co.; Lowie Museum collection.

99. WAPPO; photo by E. S. Curtis, Southwest Museum collection.

100. MIWOK; Lena Brown; photo C. Hart Merriam, Yosemite Valley, ca. 1910; Lowie Museum negative 23223.

101. MOHAVE; photo C. C. Pierce collection, Southwest Museum 3417.

102. POMO; photo E. S. Curtis, Southwest Museum collection.

103. HUPA; photo P. E. Goddard, Blocksburg, Humboldt Co., 1903; Lowie Museum negative 3026.

104. MOHAVE; C. C. Pierce collection, Southwest Museum 3409.

105. YUROK; Fanny Flounder, born 1870, died 1945; photo courtesy of Mrs. Ruth Roberts.

106. MOHAVE; Ashpram; photo A. L. Kroeber, near Needles, 1908; Lowie Museum negative 4330.

107. MOHAVE; before 1900; Southwest Museum collection.

108. MONACHE; Jack Littlefield; photo E. W. Gifford, 1922; Lowie Museum negative 6834.

109. MIWOK; Sophie Thompson; born 1868; photo E. W. Gifford, June 1923, at Tuolumne; Lowie Museum negative 7113.

110. MIWOK; Captain Eph; photo C. Hart Merriam at West Point, Calaveras Co., Aug. 1903; Lowie Museum negative 23224.

111. YUMA; G. Wharton James collection; exhibits original hair style; Southwest Museum collection.

112. JUANENO, of Mission San Juan Capistrano; Chola Martina; photo C. F. Lummis, 1907; Southwest Museum collection.

113. MOHAVE; Bluebird; photo A. L. Kroeber, 1908; Lowie Museum negative 4312.

114. YUROK; Robert Frank Spott; born 1888; Requa; Lowie Museum negative.

115. MOHAVE; Southwest Museum collection.

116. KAROK; Old Bob; photo E. S. Curtis at Orleans Bar; Southwest Museum collection 3879-B.

117. YAHI; Ishi; born ca. 1862, died 1916; Lowie Museum negative.

ACKNOWLEDGMENTS

We acknowledge with thanks permission to use pictures from the R. H. Lowie Museum, Berkeley; the C. Hart Merriam Collection, Berkeley; the American Museum of Natural History, New York City; and Mr. F. F. Latta, the foremost student of the Yokuts Indians. We also thank Lord Snowdon for permission to quote from his book, *London*, Tony Armstrong Jones, 1958, Jarrold and Sons Ltd., London; and for permission to quote at length from the *Handbook of the Indians of California*, A. L. Kroeber (first publication, Smithsonian Institution 1925) we thank G. B. Rumsey, President, California Book Co., Ltd., Berkeley, which published editions of the *Handbook* in 1958 and 1967.

It is a pleasure to declare here our particular indebtedness and thanks to the Southwest Museum, Los Angeles, to its Director, Karl Dentzel, to its Assistant Director, Bruce Bryan, and to the staff of the Museum for opening their picture files to us—some of our most treasured pictures come from those files—and for their scientifically and personally directed hospitality and cordiality.

Our debt to Hugo Rudinger of Berkeley is absolute: without him there would have been no book. As a labor of love and with loving care and infinite patience he has brought many of our pictures to the place where they were reproducible. This task took him many weeks of the most tedious and skilled photographic work.

We thank David Brower for welcoming our book to the shelves of the Sierra Club with such generous understanding and appreciation of its purpose.

We thank David Hales for his editorial criticism and for assisting us in the layout we envisioned but scarcely knew how to begin to realize.

Never have two brash authors been indebted to so many for so much. We thank them all.

THEODORA KROEBER
ROBERT F. HEIZER

ISHI

He had mastered the philosophy of patience, without trace either of self-pity, or of bitterness to dull the purity of his cheerful enduringness.

ALFRED LOUIS KROEBER

He looked upon us as sophisticated children—smart, but not wise. We knew many things, and much that is false. He knew nature, which is always true. His were the qualities of character that last forever. He was kind; he had courage and self-restraint, and though all had been taken from him, there was no bitterness in his heart. His soul was that of a child, his mind that of a philosopher.

—SAXTON T. POPE

CATALOG OF PHOTOGRAPHS

1. LAKE MIWOK, Oleyome subtribe; photo C. Hart Merriam, 1906; Lowie Museum negative 23201.
2. KAROK; Sandy Bar Bob; Orleans Bar, Humboldt Co.; photo C. Hart Merriam, Sept. 1921; Lowie Museum negative 23202.
3. SOUTHERN MAIDU (?); ca. 1850; Southwest Museum; see *Southwest Museum Masterkey*, Vol. 28, No. 5, 1954.
4. YUROK; Alice Frank Spott, 27 years old; Requa; photo 1907; Lowie Museum negative 3834.
5. YUROK; Robert Frank Spott, born 1888; Requa; photo ca. 1932; photo courtesy of Mrs. Roberts.
6. MOHAVE; C. C. Pierce collection, Southwest Museum print 3404; ca. 1900.
7. FERNANDEÑO; Rogerio Rocha, born 1801, died 1904; photo Charles F. Lummis; Southwest Museum collection.
8. COSTANOAN OF MISSION SAN JUAN BAUTISTA; Barbara Salorsano, age ca. 60; photo C. Hart Merriam, Sept. 1902; Lowie Museum negative 23203.
9. WINTUN, Napa tribelet; the last of the Napas; photo C. Hart Merriam, 1927; Lowie Museum negative 23204.
10. SOUTHERN MAIDU; Blind Tom, born ca. 1850 at village of Pusune on right bank at mouth of American River (present-day Sacramento); photo C. Hart Merriam, 1905; Lowie Museum negative 23205.
11. YOKUTS, Yachicumni subtribe; Joe Guzman, born at the Indian village in Stockton. ca. 1850, died Sept. 17, 1934; photo C. Hart Merriam, Aug. 1934; Lowie Museum negative 23206.
12. YOKUTS, Wikchumni subtribe; Wahnomkot, born 1868; photo Leon Dial, 1930; F. F. Latta collection.
13. YOKUTS, Koyeti subtribe; José Vera, born 1868; photo C. Hart Merriam at Tule River Indian Reservation, Sept. 1935; Lowie Museum negative 23207.
14. YOKUTS, Chukchansi subtribe; Mary George, born ca. 1862; photo E. W. Gifford, July 1922; Lowie Museum negative 23208.
15. YOKUTS, Wikchumni subtribe; Maggie Icho; photo 1939; Southwest Museum collection negative 1021-9.
16. LUISENO, Saboba Reservation; photo G. Wharton James, 1897; Southwest Museum collection.
17. DEGUEÑO; Manuel Lechuza; photo C. F. Lummis at Santa Ysabel Reservation, 1902. Southwest Museum collection.
18. MOHAVE; Minnie Moos; photo A. L. Kroeber, Needles, 1908; Lowie Museum negative 4322.
19. MOHAVE; photo before 1900; Southwest Museum collection.
20. YUMA; Chief Miguel; photo G. Wharton James, ca. 1900; Southwest Museum collection.
21. MOHAVE; Jack Jones (Indian name Kwaknialka); photo A. L. Kroeber, near Needles, 1908; Lowie Museum negative 4311.
22. KAROK; photo A. L. Kroeber, Aug. 1907; Lowie Museum negative 3866.
23. YUROK; Mrs. Ira Henry; photo C. Hart Merriam at Requa, Sept. 1910; Lowie Museum negative 23209.
24. YUROK; Alice Frank Spott, 27 years old; photo at Requa, 1907; Lowie Museum negative 3834.
25. YUROK; Umits, born 1844; photo A. L. Kroeber at Kepel Village on Klamath River, 1907; Lowie Museum negative 3819.
26. MOHAVE; photo ca. 1900; C. C. Pierce collection, Southwest Museum.
27. YOKUTS, Chukchansi subtribe; Nellie Graham; photo 1922; Lowie Museum negative 6861.

28. MONO PAIUTE; C. F. Saunders collection, Southwest Museum.
29. CAHUILLA; Southwest Museum collection.
30. MOHAVE; photo A. L. Kroeber, Needles, 1908; Lowie Museum negative 4327.
31. MOHAVE; photo 1907; G. Wharton James collection, Southwest Museum.
32. YOKUTS; G. Wharton James collection, Southwest Museum.
33. YUMA; G. Wharton James collection, Southwest Muesum.
34. HUPA; Lida Caesar, born 1896; photo A. L. Kroeber, 1907; Lowie Museum negative 3684.
35. MOHAVE; G. Wharton James collection, Southwest Museum.
36. YOKUTS, Gashowu subtribe; William Wesley, born 1907; photo E. W. Gifford, Fresno Co., July 1922; Lowie Museum negative 6904.
37. MIWOK, Yosemite Valley; Cozy and child; photo C. Hart Merriam, 1910; Lowie Museum negative 23210.
38. HUPA; W. Smoker and H. Campbell, born ca. 1895; photo A. L. Kroeber, 1907; Lowie Museum negative 3707.
39. MOHAVE; G. Wharton James collection, Southwest Museum.
40. ACHOMAWI; Barney Ronur, age 19; photo E. W. Gifford, 1922; Lowie Museum negative 6759.
41. MONACHE; Annie Anderson, born 1902; photo E. W. Gifford, Fresno Co., July 1922; Lowie Museum negative 6820.
42. MAIDU; Johnny Paiyute; photo R. B. Dixon, 1900; American Museum of Natural History negative 12232.
43. MOHAVE; Southwest Museum collection.
44. HUPA; Gladys Matilten, born 1892; photo A. L. Kroeber, 1907; Lowie Museum negative 3712.

45. MOHAVE; Paul; photo A. L. Kroeber, near Needles, 1908; Lowie Museum negative 4318.
46. WINTUN; Mrs. Ray Wilson, born 1898; photo E. W. Gifford, July 1922; Lowie Museum negative 6802.
47. MOHAVE; G. Wharton James collection, Southwest Museum print 5715.
48. ATSUGEWI; Hattie Brown, born 1907; photo E. W. Gifford, July 1922; Lowie Museum negative 6770.
49. ATSUGEWI; Billy Buckskin, born 1900; photo E. W. Gifford, July 1922; Lowie Museum negative 6775.
50. WASHO; Dorothy Washo, born 1892; photo E. W. Gifford, August 1922; Lowie Museum negative 7005.
51. MOHAVE; Leslie Wilbur; photo A. L. Kroeber, near Needles, 1908; Lowie Museum negative 4315.
52. CHEMEHUEVI; G. Wharton James collection, Southwest Museum collection 4377.
53. CAHUILLA; Southwest Museum collection.
54. KATO; photo E. S. Curtis, Southwest Museum collection.
55. MODOC; Ollie Hardy, Sam Riddle, Bidwell Riddle, born ca. 1892; photo S. A. Barrett, 1907; Lowie Museum negtaive 4148.
56. MAIDU; Johnny Bob, born 1880; photo R. B. Dixon, 1900; American Museum of Natural History negative 12236.
57. BANKALACHI; Dan Williams, age 62. Photo C. Hart Merriam, Sept. 1935. Lowie Museum negative 23211.
58. MOHAVE; G. Wharton James collection, Southwest Museum.
59. MIWOK; Sam Casoose Domingo; photo E. W. Gifford, 1922; Lowie Museum negative 23212.
60. MONACHE; Harry Beecher, born 1882; photo E. W. Gifford,

116. KAROK; Old Bob

Chool the Moon will be named
Chool the Sun will be named.

They will control the world
They will keep the world alive.

   —from *Annikadel*, C. HART MERRIAM

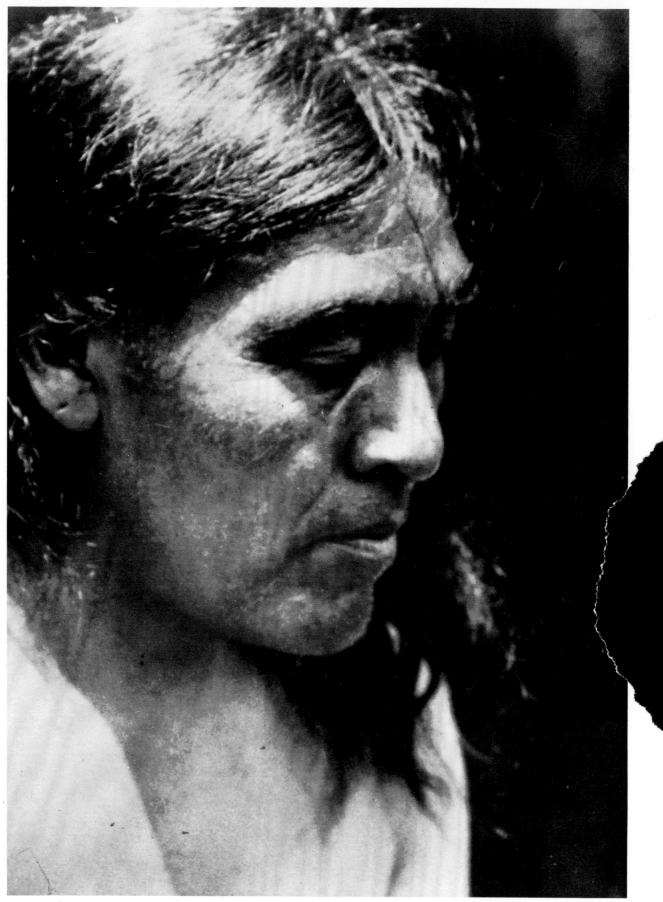

117. YAHI; Ishi, born *ca.* 1862